The House Assembly

A Guide for Recapturing
the First-Century Model
for
the Gathering of the Saints

by
Albert James Dager

SWORD PUBLISHERS

REDMOND, WASHINGTON 98073

Sword Publishers is a division of Media Spotlight Ministries

Dedicated to the King of kings and Lord of lords, true God and Savior of the world.

And to Jean, my wife and faithful companion in ministry

First Edition   April, 2004

THE HOUSE ASSEMBLY
A guide to Recapturing the First-Century Model for the Gathering of the Saints

Copyright ©2004 by Albert James Dager
Sword Publishers
P.O. Box 290
Redmond, WA 98073-0290
(425) 391-7315
www.swordpublishers.com
www.mediaspotlight.org

Library of Congress Catalog Card Number 2004092184
Trade edition ISBN 0-9626632-2-0

Contents

Introduction

In 1997 Media Spotlight published a series entitled "The Church in the Last Days," in which we stated that the time was soon coming when the establishment churches would either meld into the one-world religious milieu of the anti-Christ or cease to exist, at least openly. The alternative for true believers in Jesus would be to meet secretly in house assemblies. The series dealt extensively with the form and function of the proper assembling of believers.

At the time of that writing we saw the handwriting on the wall for the churches. Our primary focus was on how persecution might cause the Body of Christ to gather in house assemblies for survival. And while we did not wish to make a major issue of it, we recognized that most of the establishment churches have for some time been sliding into apostasy. Now that concern has grown considerably, and we are prompted to address the need for house assemblies today without regard to persecution.

Even the so-called "fundamentalist" and "evangelical" churches are taking less biblical stances on many issues. Ecumenism—unity at the expense of truth—is becoming a predominant element of church business. Psychological theories and mental manipulation have replaced ministry of the Holy Spirit in the majority of churches, including the evangelical (or, more properly, neo-evangelical) churches. On the more bizarre side, charismania is taking over many churches through "spiritual warfare" methodologies, "deliverance," and obscene manifestations falsely attributed to the Holy Spirit.

If our mail is any indication, more and more brethren are experiencing in their churches the inevitable results of religious institutionalism: abusive pastors; false teachings; church tradition; anecdotal sermons; favoritism; sinful behavior excused and even condoned, not only by favored congregants but by pastors; unaccountability of pastors; constant fund-raising for building projects; church-growth programs that suck the financial, emotional and time resources of people who feel they need to support the pastor's "vision"; and myriad other problems.

The emergence of New Thought and Higher Criticism, both of which challenge the inerrancy of Scripture, have resulted in a liberal mind-set taking over a significant number of the mainline denominations. Pentecostalism has largely fallen prey to experience-oriented mysticism, and the charismatic movement has permeated many Pentecostal and mainline Protestant denominations, as well as Roman Catholicism (which has its own problems related to doctrine and practice). Even evangelicalism, once the mainstay of sound doctrine, has succumbed to subjective religious philosophies.

Humanism and ecumenism are rapidly consuming the thoughts and energy of the established churches of every persuasion. While some admittedly hold a biblical Christology, they are basically humanistic in their understanding of, and approach to, fellowship and ministry.

A line of demarcation is being drawn daily in congregations throughout the world—particularly in the western churches. That line separates the spiritual from the carnal, faith from experience, reliance upon biblical truth from reliance upon human wisdom. Those who refuse to compromise in these areas are looked upon as unspiritual and unloving when, in fact, it is those who ostracize them for their stand that are unspiritual and unloving. As a result, many brethren are floundering in their attempts to find the fellowship and ministry they need in order to continue maturing in the Faith.

This does not mean that all these problems are in all the churches, but some if not many are found in most churches today.

Many churches exist for their own benefit rather than for the benefit of the believers. And while lip service is given to the idea that "the Church" is the people, not the building, the reality is that "the Church" is the institution—the clergy and hierarchy—not the people *or* the building (although the building is often secondary).

The majority of churches—especially the larger ones—are leaning toward a one-world, ecumenical religious system that ultimately will be the only one sanctioned by governments around the world. Those few who resist the politically-correct standards of the world's religious community will eventually be forced to conform or lose their tax-exempt status. They may even be forced into meeting in secret.

If things continue as they are the time will quickly come when we will not be able to function in the same manner to which we have become accustomed. Persecution is around the corner, and the churches that survive will be those that are willing to compromise Scripture for the sake of political correctness. Those that will not do so will find themselves forced to conform to the first-century model for the sake of survival.

In all fairness, it must be stated that there are some self-sacrificing pastors who expend their lives for the people in their care. And please don't get the idea that I'm against these men. I love those pastors who have striven against terrific pressures to minister to the brethren they genuinely love. For centuries the Lord has used them within the faulty religious systems. Some of the giants of the Faith have been such pastors. And in the past, when attending an establishment church, I have always attempted to help the pastors in any way I could. But faithful pastors are becoming fewer and fewer as many are gripped by personal ambition to rise to the status of "success" as defined by the world religious system. Church growth is the banner under which many of them operate. The more people they can get to listen to them the more successful they are perceived to be.

In the face of all these problems many believers are searching the Scriptures to find just what God would have them do. In the process they have discovered some startling truths: 1) the Body of Christ gathered together as a spiritual *family* to serve one another; 2) there were no professional, paid pastors who were preeminent above the others in the congregation; 3) a plurality of elders oversaw the assembling of the believers; 4) all elders were accountable to one another and, in truth, to all the believers in the assembly; 5) the first believers met in their homes and shared a common meal or "love feast"; 6) all were encouraged to serve as they were gifted by the Holy Spirit; 7) Jesus did not found an institution known as "the Church".

(No doubt, this last statement will have startled some, but please bear with me and you will understand exactly why I've said this.)

The churches, having come directly or indirectly out of the Roman Catholic apostasy of the fourth century, operate in opposition to the biblical model. Many believers, recognizing this, are separating themselves from the churches. This has given rise to what has come to be known as the "home church" or "house church" movement. Most within the movement use the term "home church," primarily because they are used to using the word "church" to denote the Body of Christ. Because of the connotation of the word "church" to mean a religious institution, I prefer to call the proper gathering of true believers the "house assembly."

In order to understand the proper functioning of the assembling of God's people we must begin by examining the difference between "the Church" and what Jesus really instituted—the *ekklesia* of God.

1
What is "the Church"?

When Jesus came the first time to Israel He proclaimed what He called the Gospel of the Kingdom of Heaven, also known as the Kingdom of God and the Kingdom of Christ. He spoke of how the Kingdom came in the past, how it was manifested among the Jews through His miracles, signs and wonders, how it would continue to come through the ministry of the Holy Spirit through His disciples in all ages, and will fully come in the future. There are important details to the Kingdom of Heaven which must be addressed if we are to enter into it with understanding. One of those details has to do with a great apostasy that was at work even during the time of the apostles.

Because of that apostasy, which came in the name of Jesus and claimed to be the visible representation of His Kingdom on earth, many truths about the nature of the Body of Christ have been obscured. One reason for this is that we have been taught to think of ourselves as members of something called "the Church."

Since at least as early as the fourth century, Christians have identified themselves as "the Church." We have become accustomed to the word "church," without understanding how it came about or why. This may shock some, but Jesus did not institute anything called "the Church."

But didn't Jesus say to Peter, "on this rock I will build my church"? That must prove that "the Church" is Jesus' institution.

No. Jesus said He would build His *ekklesia* (His "called out") on the faith exhibited by Peter when he stated that Jesus is the Christ (Messiah), the Son of the living God (Matthew 16:15-20).

The various English translations of Scripture use the word "church" for the Greek *ekklesia*." However, *ekklesia* is properly translated "called out." The word "church" is not a proper translation of *ekklesia*, but comes from another root word with a different meaning.

In reference to the word "Church," the *Online Etymology Dictionary* states:

> Church - O.E. *cirice* "church," from W.Gmc. **kirika*, from Gk. *kyriake (oikia)* "Lord's (house)," from *kyrios* "ruler, lord." For vowel evolution, see *bury*. Gk. *kyriakon* (adj.) "of the Lord" was used of houses of Christian worship since c.300, especially in the East, though it was less common in this sense than *ekklesia* or *basilike*. An example of the direct Gk.-to-Gmc. progress of many Christian words, via the Goths; it was probably used by W.Gmc. people in their pre-Christian period. Also picked up by Slavic, via Gmc. (cf. O.Slav. *criky*, Rus. *Cerkov*).

To explain, the term "church" (Anglo-Saxon, *cirice*, *circe*; Modern German, *cirche*; Swiss, *kyrka*) is the word employed in the Teutonic languages to translate *ekklesia*. But this is an error.

The Latin origin of the word "church" (*kyriake oikia*) means "The Lord's house." At first glance this may seem a moot point. After all, are not believers part of the Lord's house? But as it was applied to the Body of Christ by the apostate religious system, "the Lord's house" spoke of the *place* of gathering (or the institution) rather than of the people themselves who gathered. *Kyriake oikia* came to be used in the fourth century by the developing hierarchical establishment of Romanism to refer to itself and to its meeting places called "churches," "cathedrals," "chapels," etc. in which they plied their religious trade.

Another missused word is "sanctuary," the name even non-Catholic churches apply to the room in a church building where the congregation meets. The word means a holy place, or the place where God dwells. It was used for the Holy of Holies in the Hebrew temple. Yet Scripture says that each believer in Jesus is a temple of God; He does not dwell in temples made by hands (Acts 17:24; 1 Corinthians 3:16).

It's the erroneous translation of *ekklesia* that was adopted for the developing hierarchical system which eventually became the Roman Catholic Church. The carry-over of this error into the English translations of the Bible effectively keep the people thinking of themselves as members of their particular institutions rather than members of the larger Body of Christ within autonomous local assemblies.

This may be denied by religious leaders, but what do they call their institutions but "churches"? Christians ask other Christians, "Which 'church' do you attend?" Every week they attend "church." When speaking of religious meeting places even Christians encourage people to attend their "church," equivocating their church building and institution with other places of gathering such as synagogues, temples, or mosques. In practical terms, church institutions are detatched from the identity of individual believers as the *ekklesia*, or "called out" of God. Observe how they operate and you will see they exist for their own benefit above that of the people.

Although *ekklesia* may mean the "called out" for Christ in total, or as individual assemblies of the called out, it has no connotation of a religious system. It was used by the Greeks to describe any gathering of people for any number of purposes including crowds at the games. It properly means a gathering or assembly of people called out from the masses. The churches, however, are theological systems which operate on a professional level. They are clergy-laity oriented. The rank-and-file laity are distinguished from the clergy who function as priests—the perceived oracles of God. Thus, the many churches are not the true *ekklesia* of Jesus.

Outside the so-called "high" churches such as Roman Catholicism, Anglicanism, Lutheranism, and the various Orthodox churches of the East, most Christians would say that their pastors are not priests. But they make the clergy-laity distinction by referring to them as "Reverend," "Bishop," or some other hierarchical religious term. Some pastors wear clerical robes that speak as loudly as words: "I am clergy; you are laity." Even the word "pastor" is suspect. Technically, the Greek word, *poimen*, and the Latin word, *pastores*, mean "shepherds." But Latin being the official language of the apostate Roman Church, *pastores* took effect in referring to its papal priests. We need not make an issue of this fact if some prefer the word "pastor." It just helps to know.

In the true *ekklesia*, all members are equal before God, although some are gifted as elders who are to function in specific leadership roles. These are not professional clergy, but work with their own hands so that they do not become a burden to others (1 Thessalonians 4:11). Professional clergy often preach only that which is popular or will ensure their financial security.

The mistranslation of the word *ekklesia* was done to preserve the establishment of the Roman papal system. Later the practice carried over to the Reformation churches. Thus, today the word "church" is commonly used to denote the Body of Christ, whether in total, or as a local assembly. That error was further propagated by the English translators of the "New Testament," who knew that the word "church" would cement in the minds of their congregants the legitimacy of their hierarchical establishments. So, too, the words, "bishop," "pastor," and other such terms did not originate in the Greek Scriptures but in the apostate Roman Catholic religious system. All are incorrect translations of the original Greek.

This is not a matter of semantics. Those English words were included as a means to keep the people subservient to the hierarchical systems that produced their Bible translations. William Tyndale, who, from 1525 to 1535 in Germany, first translated the so-called "New Testament" into English from the Greek, rendered *ekklesia* as "congregation." Later English versions, produced by those under Church of England authority, changed it to "church." Subsequent English translations have followed suit.

In spite of these inaccuracies we can thank God for using the apostate establishments to preserve the Scriptures for us. Had it not been for their power-grabbing and avaricious nature, much of what we have in ancient manuscripts would have been lost to us today. They made possible the King James Bible and all subsequent translations in many languages for the average person. The truth is available to us if we but study the Scriptures diligently. While translations have their flaws—some more so than others—the Gospel can be found in most of them.

Because of the confusion wrought by the early apostasy, today virtually all churches hold that "the Church" was either a new creation by Jesus to replace Israel, or was created in addition to Israel as a separate entity. Both positions are based on the erroneous assumption that "the Church" was necessary to be the oracle of God because of Israel's unfaithfulness. The truth is that all the promises of God in all the books of Scripture are only to Israel, and all believers in Jesus are heirs to those promises regardless of their national heritage. This is important to know if we are going to understand the true nature of the *ekklesia* of God and function in the manner for which He has ordained us.

Read the following portion carefully and test it against the Scriptures. The truths of God's Word in relation to what is said here will set us free from the religious errors that have kept us blinded to our true inheritance in Jesus Christ.

OLD AND NEW RECONCILED

It is supposed that the "New Testament" replaced the "Old Testament" for Christians. The word rendered "testament" is *diatheke*, which means "contract." Confusion was created by those who compiled the Scriptures—particularly those within the Roman Catholic Church. That confusion exists in what is meant by the "Old Testament" and the "New Testament" as they relate to the Old Covenant and the New Covenant.

There is no such division of Scripture as an "Old Testament" and a "New Testament," except as invented by the apostate early "Church." There is only God's Word given through His prophets who wrote prior to the coming of

Israel's Messiah, and to His apostles and prophets who wrote after the coming of Israel's Messiah. There is one Testimony—the Testimony of Yeshua, HaMashiach (Jesus, the Christ), which is made up of all the prophetic writings. That Testimony was given to Israel and prophesied of the Messiah before He appeared (the pre-messianic Scriptures), and related His life and teachings after He appeared (the post-messianic Scriptures).

"The Church" separated these into two categories called "Old Testament" and "New Testament," then said that these are two different covenants for two different people—the "old" for the Jews, the "new" for "the Church".

Since "testament" means "covenant," it was erroneous for them to separate the prophetic writings given before Messiah came, from the prophetic writings given after Messiah came, and call them the "Old Testament" and the "New Testament." This implied that all of the pre-messianic writings comprised the whole of what was done away with when Messiah instituted His New Covenant in His blood. Yet the only parts of those pre-messianic writings that were done away with were specific Mosaic laws given to Israel to keep them separated from the nations and to provide for atonement from sin until Messiah came. But it is not true of God's original covenant with Abraham, or of any other Scriptures.

The pre-messianic Scriptures recorded many covenants with different people: Adam and Eve, Noah, Abraham, Isaac, Jacob, and others, including non-Israelites such as Hagar and her son Ishmael (Genesis 17:20). So the so-called "Old Testament" is really the record of many testaments (covenants) between God and men. All of those covenants were specific to those people.

The Old Covenant in Moses, and the New Covenant in Jesus, were made specifically with the house of Israel. The Old Covenant was sealed by keeping the Law by faith. The New Covenant with the house of Israel was sealed with the blood of Messiah. All who come to Him enter into the covenant God made with Abraham. That Covenant is not part of the Old Covenant which Jesus said is done away with. Only the Old

Covenant with Israel through Moses has been done away with and replaced by the New Covenant in Jesus' blood. Therefore, the only parts of the pre-messianic writings that do not apply to today's Israel of Faith are those that specifically related to Israel's sacrifices for sin and separation from the nations, the ceremonial laws that pointed to the future coming of Messiah, and certain covenants made with certain individuals. Once Messiah fulfilled the Mosaic laws they no longer had to be adhered to by faithful Israel. The wall of separation was torn down and the Gentiles were invited to enter into the New Covenant with Israel.

The Abrahamic covenant has been misunderstood and/or ignored for centuries to the detriment of the spiritual growth of Christians. While the New Covenant replaced the Mosaic Covenant, it did not replace the Abrahamic Covenant. It supplements the Abrahamic Covenant. And since the promise was to Abraham, Isaac and Jacob, the New Covenant pertains to Israel, not to "the Church." This is borne out in the Scriptures.

When Jesus told His apostles at His Passover meal prior to going to the cross, "This is my blood of the new testament [covenant], which is shed for many," He was fulfilling a prophecy given through Jeremiah that spoke of a new covenant God would make, not with some new entity called "the Church," but with *Israel*:

> *Behold, the days come, saith the LORD, that __I will make a new covenant with the house of Israel, and with the house of Judah__:*
>
> *Not according to the covenant that I made with their fathers in the day that I took them by the hand to bring them out of the land of Egypt; which my covenant they brake, although I was an husband unto them, saith the LORD:*
>
> *But this shall be the covenant that __I will make with the house of Israel__; After those days, saith the LORD, I will put my law in their inward parts, and write it in their hearts; and will be their God, and they shall be my people.* (Jeremiah 31:31-33)

This prophecy pertained to Jesus at His first coming. It is specific to the ten tribes of Israel and the two tribes of Judah. That specificity means it cannot be construed to mean that the New Covenant was made with some new entity called "the Church," which ostensibly replaced, or was created in addition to, Israel. This is affirmed in the post-messianic Scriptures, especially in the writing to the Hebrew believers in Jesus. Speaking of Jesus as the perfect High Priest of Israel, the writer refers to Jeremiah's prophecy:

> But now hath he obtained a more excellent ministry, by how much also he is the mediator of a better covenant, which was established upon better promises.
>
> For if that first covenant had been faultless, then should no place have been sought for the second.
>
> For finding fault with them, he saith, Behold, the days come, saith the Lord, when _I will make a new covenant with the house of Israel and with the house of Judah_:
>
> Not according to the covenant that I made with their fathers in the day when I took them by the hand to lead them out of the land of Egypt; because they continued not in my covenant, and I regarded them not, saith the Lord.
>
> For this is the covenant that _I will make with the house of Israel_ after those days, saith the Lord; I will put my laws into their mind, and write them in their hearts: and I will be to them a God, and they shall be to me a people:
>
> And they shall not teach every man his neighbour, and every man his brother, saying, Know the Lord: for all shall know me, from the least to the greatest.
>
> For I will be merciful to their unrighteousness, and their sins and their iniquities will I remember no more.
>
> In that he saith, A new covenant, he hath made the first old. Now that which decayeth and waxeth old is ready to vanish away. (Hebrews 8:6-13)

The Old Covenant was that which God made with Israel through Moses and the giving of the Mosaic laws. That covenant provided for animal sacrifices which could not fully remove the sins of the people. They had to be performed over and over again, and were merely types that pointed to the perfect sacrifice of Jesus Christ on the cross of Calvary.

The New Covenant is a more perfect one based upon the shed blood of Jesus. **Both the Old Covenant and New Covenant are said to be made with "the house of Israel and the house of Judah."** Thus, the imperfect was replaced by the perfect for the benefit of Israel which, in its totality, included Judah and Benjamin—the house of Judah. There is no mention of "the Church."

God's covenant with Abraham through Israel still stands; only the aspects of the covenant given through Moses and pertaining to sacrifices for sin, and those meant to keep Israel separate from the nations are done away with.

While the Mosaic laws pertaining to the sacrifices and other things necessary to demonstrate righteousness before God were done away with, it remains that God's covenant with Abraham, operating through Israel, carries through to the disciples of Jesus. This is part of the Gospel: we are joint heirs with Christ as promised to the father of our faith, Abraham. This is affirmed in the post-messianic Scriptures:

> *Even as Abraham believed God, and it was accounted to him for righteousness.*
>
> *Know ye therefore that they which are of faith, the same are the children of Abraham.*
>
> *And the scripture, foreseeing that God would justify the heathen through faith, preached before the gospel unto Abraham, saying, In thee shall all nations be blessed.*
>
> *So then they which be of faith are blessed with faithful Abraham....*
>
> *Christ hath redeemed us from the curse of the law, being made a curse for us: for it is written, Cursed is every one that hangeth on a tree:*

> *That the blessing of Abraham might come on the*
> *Gentiles through Jesus Christ; that we might receive*
> *the promise of the Spirit through faith....*
> *Now to Abraham and his seed were the promises*
> *made. He saith not, And to seeds, as of many; but as of*
> *one, And to thy seed, which is Christ.* (Galatians
> 3:6-16)

Thus, we enter not into the Mosaic Covenant, but into the
Abrahamic Covenant. Now believers from all nations are joined
with the faithful of Israel so that out of the two, God has made
one people for Himself (Ephesians 2:15). The Abrahamic
Covenant was not annulled by the Mosaic Covenant:

> *And this I say, that the covenant, that was*
> *confirmed before of God in Christ, the law, which was*
> *four hundred and thirty years after, cannot disannul,*
> *that it should make the promise of none effect.*
> *For if the inheritance be of the law, it is no more of*
> *promise: but God gave it to Abraham by promise.*
> (Galatians 3:17-18)

To whom was the promise of a better covenant given? It
was given to Israel. Yet all who come to Christ by faith, whether
born to Israel or to other nations, are heirs of the Abrahamic
Covenant:

> *For ye are all the children of God by faith in Christ*
> *Jesus.*
> *For as many of you as have been baptized into*
> *Christ have put on Christ.*
> *There is neither Jew nor Greek, there is neither*
> *bond nor free, there is neither male nor female: for ye*
> *are all one in Christ Jesus.*
> *And if ye be Christ's, then are ye Abraham's seed, and*
> *heirs according to the promise.* (Galatians 3:26-29)

Why, if "the Church" replaced, or is distinct from, Israel,
did the apostles affirm to Gentile believers God's promises to
Abraham?

God said that through Abraham all nations would be blessed (Galatians 3:8). Isaiah said he would be a light to the Gentiles:

> *And he said, It is a light thing that thou shouldest be my servant to raise up the tribes of Jacob, and to restore the preserved of Israel: I will also give thee for a light to the Gentiles, that thou mayest be my salvation unto the end of the earth.* (Isaiah 49:6)

The promise is to Israel first, and then to the Gentiles. Simeon, seeing the child Jesus in the temple reiterated Isaiah:

> *For mine eyes have seen thy salvation,*
> *Which thou hast prepared before the face of all people;*
> *A light to lighten the Gentiles, and the glory of thy people Israel.* (Luke 2:30-32)

Jesus came to break down the wall of separation between Israel and the other nations:

> *Wherefore remember, that ye being in time past Gentiles in the flesh, who are called Uncircumcision by that which is called the Circumcision in the flesh made by hands;*
> *That at that time ye were without Christ, being aliens from the commonwealth of Israel, and strangers from the covenants of promise, having no hope, and without God in the world:*
> *But now in Christ Jesus ye who sometimes were far off are made nigh by the blood of Christ.*
> *For he is our peace, who hath made both one, and hath broken down the middle wall of partition between us.*
> *Having abolished in his flesh the enmity, even the law of commandments contained in ordinances; for to make in himself of twain one new man, so making peace;*
> *And that he might reconcile both unto God in one body by the cross, having slain the enmity thereby:*

And came and preached peace to you which were
afar off, and to them that were nigh.
For through him we both have access by one Spirit
unto the Father.
Now therefore ye are no more strangers and
foreigners, but fellowcitizens with the saints, and of
the household of God;
And are built upon the foundation of the apostles
and prophets, Jesus Christ himself being the chief
corner stone. (Ephesians 2:11-20)

The Gentiles, without Christ, are alienated from the
commonwealth of Israel and are strangers from the covenant of
promise. In Christ they are bonded to the commonweath of
Israel and partake of the New Covenant. At the same time, the
unbelieving Israelites are cut off from the commonwealth of
Israel. This is a mystery that was hidden throughout the ages:

Whereof I am made a minister, according to the
dispensation of God which is given to me for you, to
fulfil the word of God;
Even the mystery which hath been hid from ages
and from generations, but now is made manifest to his
saints:
To whom God would make known what is the
riches of the glory of this mystery among the Gentiles;
which is Christ in you, the hope of glory. (Colossians
1:25-27)

So sacred is the truth that God has made of two people one
in Israel for His glory, that Paul condemns those who would
erect again the wall of separation torn down through Christ's
sacrifice:

But when Peter was come to Antioch, I withstood
him to the face, because he was to be blamed.
For before that certain came from James, he did eat
with the Gentiles: but when they were come, he
withdrew and separated himself, fearing them which
were of the circumcision.

And the other Jews dissembled likewise with him; insomuch that Barnabas also was carried away with their dissimulation.

But when I saw that they walked not uprightly according to the truth of the gospel, I said unto Peter before them all, If thou, being a Jew, livest after the manner of Gentiles, and not as do the Jews, why compellest thou the Gentiles to live as do the Jews?

We who are Jews by nature, and not sinners of the Gentiles,

Knowing that a man is not justified by the works of the law, but by the faith of Jesus Christ, even we have believed in Jesus Christ, that we might be justified by the faith of Christ, and not by the works of the law: for by the works of the law shall no flesh be justified. (Galatians 2:11-16)

From the very beginning, Satan tried to undo what Christ had done. He tried to drive a wedge between Israel and the Gentiles, devising false teachings that treated the two as something distinct.

Roman Catholicism proved his perfect foil to accomplish this. Using the military power of Rome, the religious system—a hybrid Christian-pagan hierarchical "church"—imposed upon kings and their subjects the belief that the Kingdom of God had come through the Roman pontiff as the Vicar of Christ on earth. Its leaders claimed that Israel was no longer the inheritor of God's promises; "the Church" was. Thus, "the Church" drove further the wedge between the two through persecution and a bloody pogrom.

Although God has preserved individuals in the Christian religious institutions, the fact remains that those institutions are all illegitimate usurpers of the promises made to the Israel of Faith. They do not proclaim the full Gospel, but claim rewards and promises distinct from those of the Israel of Faith. In so doing, they cut off their hearers from blessings.

It pains me to say this. I know wonderful men who are pastors of the churches I am indicting. I would not question their love for the Lord. They also are victims of the deception, having been trained in particular theological systems. I know I am wounding them by my words here. All I can say is I'm sorry. But as I understood these things I felt the same as when the true nature of the Roman Catholic Church—which I loved—was revealed to me in 1964. I gave up what I loved for Him whom I loved more.

To be sure, we are not saved by this knowledge. We are saved by grace through faith in the Son of God. And we must regard as saved by grace our true brethren in Christ who are still in the churches, content under the tutelage of even the most errant pastors. We must likewise regard as saved those pastors who labor out of a motive of love for God's flock. We cannot be prideful of this knowledge. Our eyes may be opened now, but they were closed for too long before. Let us show grace toward those who do not yet see these truths. Some may resist until they are cast out of the churches. Some pastors will be cast out by their congregations when they begin to really minister the truth as well.

WERE JESUS' WORDS FOR "THE CHURCH"?

Satan had such great success in erecting again the wall of separation through the churches that there are some who even say that Jesus' words were not meant for "the Church," but were part of the "Old Covenant" for the Jews only.

They assume that since the Lord related His teachings to the Law, they were meant only for Israel. And since the Law was done away with, they do not apply to "the Church." They assume that Israel was saved by keeping the Law while "the Church" is saved by grace merely through affirmation of faith in Jesus. They have misconstrued the meaning of grace, lacking understanding of how grace came to Israel through the Law, and have established an inadequate gospel as a means to salvation.

Let us be clear about this very important truth: there is nothing man can do to earn his salvation. Salvation comes by grace through faith, and that is a gift from God (Ephesians 2:4-10). God's gift of faith is available to all who seek truth with an honest heart:

O Lord, open thou my lips; and my mouth shall shew forth thy praise.

For thou desirest not sacrifice; else would I give it: thou delightest not in burnt offering.

The sacrifices of God are a broken spirit: a broken and a contrite heart, O God, thou wilt not despise. (Psalms 51:15-17)

Many assert that man's heart is utterly corrupt, and that no semblance of goodness can be found in it. True, there are several Scriptures that attest to the deceitfulness of man's heart in general. Yet man, bearing the image of God, does have a modicum of goodness, even if that goodness of itself cannot save him. Even Jesus, when explaining the parable of the sower, acknowledged the possibility of men possessing an honest and good heart:

But that on the good ground are they, which in an honest and good heart, having heard the word, keep it, and bring forth fruit with patience. (Luke 8:15)

So whom do we believe? Jesus or some theological system? I suppose we should correct the Lord?

We are saved by God's grace, not by our own works of righteousness. But our response to God's grace reveals the condition of our hearts. We are not robots to be forced against our wills into the Kingdom of Heaven. We have the ability to choose Christ or reject Him. Otherwise there would be no such thing as love on our part toward our heavenly Father and Jesus. Love is an act of one's will. And God desires that we love Him with all our heart, soul, strength and mind.

God's grace as the only means of salvation does not apply only to Jesus' disciples, but also to pre-messianic Israel. Israelites were never saved by keeping the Law; faith has always been at the heart of God's dealing with men even from the creation of Adam. The moral law was given to Israel as an expression of God's grace to show man what God required of him in order to be in fellowship with Him. It was never meant as a way to be saved.

True faith desires to obey God's moral law, which must be kept by faith in what it teaches us: that God has made us His workmanship, created in Christ Jesus to do good works in which God had ordained us to walk. One cannot break God's commands and claim to love God. Jesus said, "If ye love me, keep my commandments" (John 14:15).

"But," some say, "Jesus was not speaking to the Church, He spoke only to Israel." Yet what did He say immediately following?

> *If ye love me, keep my commandments.*
> *And I will pray the Father, and he shall give you another Comforter, that he may abide with you for ever;*
> *Even the Spirit of truth; whom the world cannot receive, because it seeth him not, neither knoweth him: but ye know him; for he dwelleth with you, and shall be in you.*
> *I will not leave you comfortless: I will come to you.*
> *Yet a little while, and the world seeth me no more; but ye see me: because I live, ye shall live also.*
> *At that day ye shall know that I am in my Father, and ye in me, and I in you.*
> *He that hath my commandments, and keepeth them, he it is that loveth me: and he that loveth me shall be loved of my Father, and I will love him, and will manifest myself to him.* (John 14:15-21)

Those who say Jesus' words are not for "the Church" want to claim this promise of the Holy Spirit for themselves, but they do not want to assume the responsibilities required to receive that blessing. To whom has the Comforter—the Holy Spirit—been sent? To Israel, or to "the Church"? We cannot have it both ways.

In truth, the Holy Spirit is sent to those who are faithful among the Israelites and to all Gentiles who are grafted into Israel by faith in Jesus. So in that sense the Lord's words were only for Israel. And, if so, none of His words, or the words of the apostles, apply to anything called "the Church." We are all

Israel by faith if we have been baptized into the New Covenant which was promised to Israel. Thus, all of the apostles' writings are for the Israel of Faith, not for the apostate religious system that came to be known as "the Church." Additionally, those Israelites who do not believe in Jesus as their Messiah are cut off from Israel.

All who believe in Jesus as Messiah, whether Jews or Gentiles, have the faith of Abraham. And only those who have the same faith Abraham had may enter into the Kingdom of Heaven.

DOES "THE CHURCH" EXIST?

The truth is that there is no such thing as "the Church" in God's economy. All of the churches that exist today are descended from the original apostate system, no matter how far from the original they may have progressed. As long as they think of themselves as something other than a company of people within Israel, and/or as having replaced Israel, they are in error. This does not mean that all individuals in those churches are not saved, or do not love God. It merely means that they have not been taught properly who they are in Christ. God did not create a new entity to replace Israel, nor did He establish a new creation in addition to Israel. There is only the Israel of Faith which includes all the saints of all the ages, both Jew and Gentile.

I realize I am being redundant, but this is necessary to dispell the myths foisted upon the reader by his church, and to impress upon him the truth that all who would be saved, whether Jew or Gentile, are of one and the same company—Israel—through faith in the promises to Abraham:

> *Now to Abraham and his seed were the promises made. He saith not, And to seeds, as of many; but as of one, And to thy seed, which is Christ.*
>
> *And this I say, that the covenant, that was confirmed before of God in Christ, the law, which was four hundred and thirty years after, cannot disannul, that it should make the promise of none effect.*

> *For if the inheritance be of the law, it is no more of promise: but God gave it to Abraham by promise....*
>
> *For ye are all the children of God by faith in Christ Jesus.*
>
> *For as many of you as have been baptized into Christ have put on Christ.*
>
> *There is neither Jew nor Greek, there is neither bond nor free, there is neither male nor female: for ye are all one in Christ Jesus.*
>
> *And if ye be Christ's, then are ye Abraham's seed, and heirs according to the promise.* (Galatians 3:16-29)

All true believers, whether born to natural Israelite stock, or to other nations, grow together on the same tree—Israel.

> *For if the firstfruit be holy, the lump is also holy: and if the root be holy, so are the branches.*
>
> *And if some of the branches be broken off, and thou, being a wild olive tree, wert graffed in among them, and with them partakest of the root and fatness of the olive tree;*
>
> *Boast not against the branches. But if thou boast, thou bearest not the root, but the root thee.*
>
> *Thou wilt say then, The branches were broken off, that I might be graffed in.*
>
> *Well; because of unbelief they were broken off, and thou standest by faith. Be not highminded, but fear:*
>
> *For if God spared not the natural branches, take heed lest he also spare not thee.*
>
> *Behold therefore the goodness and severity of God: on them which fell, severity; but toward thee, goodness, if thou continue in his goodness: otherwise thou also shalt be cut off.*
>
> *And they also, if they abide not still in unbelief, shall be graffed in: for God is able to graff them in again.*
>
> *For if thou wert cut out of the olive tree which is wild by nature, and wert graffed contrary to nature into a good olive tree: how much more shall these,*

which be the natural branches, be graffed into their own olive tree?

For I would not, brethren, that ye should be ignorant of this mystery, lest ye should be wise in your own conceits; that blindness in part is happened to Israel, until the fulness of the Gentiles be come in.

And so all Israel shall be saved: as it is written, There shall come out of Sion the Deliverer, and shall turn away ungodliness from Jacob:

For this is my covenant unto them, when I shall take away their sins. (Romans 11:16-27)

Read those Scripture verses carefully. You will see that there are not two trees, but one. God did not create a new tree called "the Church," but grafted into the existing tree, Israel (not natural Israel, but faithful Israel), all who have faith in Jesus Christ and obey His commandments by faith.

The concept of "replacement theology" is a terrible deception. It boasts against the natural branches. It states that God has completely finished with Israel with the coming of Christ, and that He has replaced Israel with something called "the Church," which word is not found in the original Greek Scriptures. As we have seen, the Greek word mistranslated "church" is *ekklesia*, which means "called out." Israel was called out from among the nations to present the Gospel to the world. This is why Paul calls the faithful of Israel "the elect of grace" (Romans 11:5). This is a term we often hear applied to the so-called "Church," but it initially applied to the believing remnant of Israel. If Paul referred to Israel as the elect of grace at a time when "the Church" was supposed to have replaced Israel, why has the concept been discarded?

Satan's hatred for God's people caused him to devise a religious system that would confuse those who come to Christ, and would obscure their understanding of the great promises that are theirs if they will be faithful.

Today, the Israel of Faith has been in captivity to pastoral Christianity for the past 1700 years, just as it was in captivity to rabbinic Judaism for centuries before the Messiah came. In many ways pastoral Christianity is much the same as rabbinic Judaism. A remnant of rabbis followed their Messiah when He came. Most rejected Him. A remnant of pastors strive to remain faithful to the Lord. Most do not. And most in both companies have made the Scriptures of no effect in the lives of God's Israel through their traditions. If there *are* two distinct companies *they are Judaism and Christianity,* both of which are part of the world's religious system. Many of today's Christian leaders do not realize the degree to which worldly tradition governs their belief systems.

Should we be surprised that they are sliding into apostasy, considering that they originated in apostasy?

What is written in these pages is not a "new revelation" in the sense of extra-biblical "knowledge." It is just better understanding of the knowledge already contained in Scripture.

Certainly others must have seen these truths. Perhaps some in the messianic congregations have seen them, although most do not consider biblical Christianity a continuation of biblical Judaism. (Actually, there is no such thing as "biblical Christianity" or "biblical Judaism." There is only the biblical Faith once delivered to the saints.) The churches think it is their duty to make "Christians" out of Jews and bring them into "the Church"—their institutions.

On the other side, many messianic congregations believe that God has two ways of dealing with His people: one way for naturally born Israelites, another way for those grafted into Israel by faith in Messiah Jesus. They want us to believe that they are our mentors because of their natural heritage. Yet what they offer is not the true Faith alone, but a Christianized form of rabbinic Judaism, some even insisting on the keeping of the Mosaic law, at least for those born as natural Israelites.

So both the churches and the messianic congregations are rebuilding the wall of separation that Jesus tore down.

It is permissible for Jesus' disciples to put themselves under the Law in order to win those under the Mosaic law as Paul did (1 Corinthians 9:19-23). But that is the extent of having any legitimate thing to do with the Law. Let us keep the Covenant in His blood as one people in Christ.

I am certain that many who read this will be alarmed. It's as if the very foundation for all they have believed since coming to Christ has been taken out from under them. That is how I felt when the truth about Roman Catholicism was revealed to me. At that time I determined to leave that place of comfort—of beloved priests and comfortable ritual. I knew that I could not remain there and be faithful to the Lord because of the truth I had attained.

RELIGIOUS OPPOSITION

The house assembly movement does not sit well with religious people—especially religious leaders—who enjoy the preeminence among their flocks. Criticism will abound against the "unscholarly" elders—men who bear no initials after their names—who do not assume the titles, "Reverend," "Most Right Reverend," or "bishop."

Like most of my statements in this writing, this should not be taken as a blanket condemnation. Many credentialed men are godly seekers after truth and serve the brethren faithfully. These will not take offense, nor will they take pride in their credentials, recognizing that the pope has credentials, as does Bishop Spong and all the participants in the nefarious Jesus Seminar, as well as church leaders who promote homosexual marriages and homosexual leadership in the churches.

However, the religious establishment in general doesn't acknowledge the spiritual leadership of "uncredentialed" men. It does not afford the Holy Spirit His due in being able to teach the humble in spirit or to guide them in ministry (1 John 2:27).

The name of the game for the religious establishment is control and self-glorification. And if an assembly does not have the government-approved 501 (c) 3 tax-exempt status, or has not been born from a larger organization that does, it is looked upon as a cult or, at best, a group of unruly miscreants, unworthy of consideration for holding truth.

Contrary to this elitist mind-set, credentials are far less important than the fruit of the Spirit being manifested among an assembly's elders. They prove nothing more than that those who receive them have been approved by a theological system.

God's words are as true for many of today's pastors as they were for Israel's shepherds in Ezekiel's day:

*And the word of the L*ord *came unto me, saying,*

*Son of man, prophesy against the shepherds of Israel, prophesy, and say unto them, Thus saith the Lord G*od *unto the shepherds; Woe be to the shepherds of Israel that do feed themselves! should not the shepherds feed the flocks?*

Ye eat the fat, and ye clothe you with the wool, ye kill them that are fed: but ye feed not the flock.

The diseased have ye not strengthened, neither have ye healed that which was sick, neither have ye bound up that which was broken, neither have ye brought again that which was driven away, neither have ye sought that which was lost; but with force and with cruelty have ye ruled them.

And they were scattered, because there is no shepherd: and they became meat to all the beasts of the field, when they were scattered.

My sheep wandered through all the mountains, and upon every high hill: yea, my flock was scattered upon all the face of the earth, and none did search or seek after them.

*Therefore, ye shepherds, hear the word of the L*ord*;*

*As I live, saith the Lord G*od*, surely because my flock became a prey, and my flock became meat to every beast of the field, because there was no shepherd, neither did my shepherds search for my flock, but the shepherds fed themselves, and fed not my flock;*

*Therefore, O ye shepherds, hear the word of the L*ord*;*

*Thus saith the Lord G*od*; Behold, I am against the shepherds; and I will require my flock at their hand, and cause them to cease from feeding the flock; neither shall the shepherds feed themselves any more; for I will deliver my flock from their mouth, that they may not be meat for them.* (Ezekiel 34:1-8)

Yet, just as there were a few faithful shepherds at that time, so there are a few today. The sad thing is that the unfaithful shepherds will not recognize themselves in these words. They think that the Lord is speaking only to the Christ-denying clergy in liberal churches. But, in fact, He is speaking to all who hold man's teachings in higher regard than Scripture—even when man's teachings seemingly conform to Scripture.

Regard for man's teachings above Scripture is learned in seminaries and Bible colleges that teach theological systems rather than the pure, unadulterated biblical truth of God's Word. They teach pastors how to control their congregations rather than how to serve them. They stress the need for credentials for anyone—man or woman—who would take any significant leadership in a church body. They incorporate psychological theories and other forms of human wisdom to create a hybrid religious system, all the while genuinely thinking they are being faithful to God.

Because today's pastors are like those in Ezekiel's time, God is bringing judgment upon the churches. That judgment is taking the form of a strong delusion which will try the hearts of many—a delusion so great that, if it were possible, even the very elect would be deceived (Matthew 24:24). How sad that our Lord's warnings go largely unheeded by those who think they can own truth apart from Scripture.

The days of comfort are ended; the days of tribulation lie ahead. How will the majority of Christians react to God's judgment upon the churches? Sadly, the majority will resist correction. They will defend their pastors who abuse them because much of the abuse is not severe or palpable; it is spiritual rather than temporal.

Today's abuse is characterized by the deprivation of truth as well as by unscriptural demands. In the minds of religious leaders the deprivation of truth is not as important as the deprivation of social programs. But this is as Jesus said:

> *Woe unto the world because of offences! for it must needs be that offences come; but woe to that man by whom the offence cometh!* (Matthew 18:7)

SHOULD YOU LEAVE YOUR CHURCH?

Now the question arises whether or not everyone should leave their churches and all the comfort they provide. They love those with whom they fellowship. They know that salvation is in Jesus, not in the church they attend. They love their pastors, and rightly so. They should not forget the true servants of God who have labored in the churches these past centuries—some still today. But they also know that the church system is part of the world's religious establishment, its various elements at worst controlled by Satan; at best influenced by him.

If you are blessed to be in a loving fellowship guided by a godly pastor, perhaps you will find that this writing isn't for you, at least at this time. Or if you are a pastor whose heart is toward God and you recognize the deceptions that are prevalent in most of today's churches, perhaps you will see some things that will encourage you toward even more biblical orientation.

Each must make up his own mind what to do, provided his church is not overtly apostate. However, for those with knowledge the purpose for attending should shift from what they can receive from the churches to what they have to offer to the churches in the way of sharing the truth. We should treat the churches as the Lord's disciples treated the synagogues. Recognize that few in them hold a genuine faith in the Lord, but demonstrate the love of Christ to all.

Yet we should not be naïve to think that the words of truth we bring will be welcomed. Jesus told His disciples that He was sending them out as sheep among wolves (Matthew 10:16-17). He warned that they would be cast out of the synagogues and would even be killed by those who think they are doing God a service (John 16:2).

It is difficult to face the prospect of giving up one's church. The churches provide a sense of community; they give an air of security; they are lovely places. And there are many sweet brethren in them. But the cost of following Christ is to be willing to give up one's own life for Him.

I am not suggesting my brethren do anything more than I have done. I know the pain that arises with separation from those we love.

Frankly, the chances are good that you will not need to leave your church on your own; just start ministering the hard truth, start calling into question some of the unbiblical teachings and practices, and most likely you will be escorted out.

You can be sure most of the churches will say we are apostate, even reprobate—that we hate Christians and Christianity. They will warn others that we are a cult, and that they should stay away from us. They will demand to see our "credentials," just as Israel's religious leaders demanded of the Lord and His disciples their credentials. Yet the myriad theologians of the Christian religions all have credentials and they cannot agree on what is the truth. But they will join with one another against us in spite of their disagreements because they possess the same religious spirit. They have a large investment in their religious systems and they won't like seeing them threatened.

What they will not do is weigh by the Scriptures what we have to say, at least not without scouring commentaries and theological theses in vain attempts to support their position and assuage their consciences.

THE DIFFERENCE

One very important thing: Because Christians have been conditioned to think of "the Church" as their home, and church buildings as their authorized place of gathering, they will not understand just what a Holy Spirit-led house assembly really is.

Even those who have forsaken the formal church setting in favor of the house assembly have a difficult time thinking of their gathering as that of the family of God—the *ekklesia*. So let us make clear what our gatherings are not. They are not "Bible-study groups," "Bible fellowships," "cell churches," "care groups," social gatherings for Christians or anything less than or different from the assembly of the saints just as were the first-century gatherings described in Scripture.

It is important that we stop using the word "church" to describe ourselves or our gatherings lest we fail to make the distinction in our own minds, let alone in the minds of others. Thus, you will notice that in the Scriptures we quote in this book we have replaced the mistranslation of the word "church" with the word "assembly" in keeping with the traditional Greek usage. For reasons explained in later chapters, we also have replaced the mistranslation of the word *episkopon* as "bishop" with "overseer," which is synonymous with *presbuteros*— "elder." This is to distinguish between the commonly held error that a "bishop" is some hierarchical figure within an institution known as a "church."

We must also stand ready to correct those who have these false impressions because of their ignorance. Help them see that our Father has a more excellent way of gathering—free from the constraints of religious men and women—wherein every member of the body may be fitly joined together and compacted by that which every joint supplies, according to the effectual working in the measure of every part, making increase of the body unto the edifying of itself in love. (Ephesians 4:16)

It will take time for things to come together as the Lord intended. We carry a lot of baggage out of the churches. But patient enduring of our stumbling along the path to biblical fellowship will eventually be rewarded.

In the process of our learning anew what God intends for His called out ones, it's important that we not paint all churches and all pastors with the broad brushstroke of heresy merely because we may perceive that they are operating under an institutional system. Therefore, I offer in a spirit of love and with the desire to help, what I believe the Lord has been placing upon my heart for His people in these last days.

I look upon these suggestions as the ideal, gleaned from many hours of Scripture study during some forty years of walking with the Lord. Not to mention my first twenty-five years having been raised in the Roman Catholic Church. But I also recognize that some of the things offered may not work for some. My only request is that the reader approach what I have to say with an open mind and an open Bible.

2

The Pattern

The movement away from institutional religion is not an organizational one, but a generally autonomous response to a growing disenchantment and frustration with the institutional churches experienced by many believers in Jesus. This disenchantment and frustration has grown more acute as believers mature in their understanding of Scripture. Even as independent churches have sprung up in the past in response to the formal and formulaic approach of the mainline denominations, so house assemblies are springing up in response to what some see as the "same-old, same-old" aspects of the independent churches, as well as of the mainline denominations.

This movement eschews the formality of the church service and seeks more intimate, Holy Spirit-led ministry that encourages spiritual growth in the biblical sense. This pattern, I believe, is a step in the right direction.

But there are issues even with the house assembly movement that must be addressed if the believer is to find true biblical fellowship.

To begin, anything that becomes a "movement" carries with it diverse issues wherein the people involved try to exert their particular beliefs and practices. Even autonomous movements risk becoming stagnated and/or turned into another denomination, or at least affiliation, which tends to exert outside influence upon the individual assemblies. It is our desire to offer some guidelines and resources to help those who may be seeking more biblical ministry than they are finding in their present church.

While the movement has taken on the name of "home church," or "house church," implying that private homes are the only place to meet, some which have grown too large for the home do meet in public buildings. It isn't so much where the Body of Christ meets as it is the form and function of the gathering that is important. It is for this reason, as well as the fact that even some house gatherings depart from the purity of the faith, that I choose to call the proper assembling of the "called-out" (*ekklesia*), "the Lord's assembly" or "house assembly." This with the understanding that it will generally meet in the homes of the brethren who form them. This may seem a minor point, but the word "church," remember, refers to the religious institutions. I also prefer the term "house assembly" to "home church," because people often refer to their institutional church as their "home church," especially when traveling. Also, home churches have often formed the basis for a clergy-laity model which eventually sees the "need" to erect a church building.

Also, we must restate the difference between the *ekklesia*—the true assembly of believers—and so-called "cell churches" which are house groups attached to institutional churches. The Lord's assemblies are autonomous, whereas cell churches are sub-groups within institutional churches. Also, the Lord's assemblies are not confined to the oversight of a church's pastor or pastor-appointed leader. Nor does the ministry within the Lord's assemblies revolve around the pastor's weekly sermon, which is common for many cell groups.

While some of the needs for more intimate ministry are realized within both the Lord's assemblies and the cell-groups, the personal concerns and needs are shared equally within the Lord's assemblies. There are no counseling sessions set up with the pastor as someone to whom the rank-and-file look for guidance. They are not going to be exposed to others outside the gathering as could happen within the cell-group which, by its nature, is accountable to the church leadership. Since everyone within the Lord's assembly knows everyone else, and gathers together as a family, there is less concern for embarrassment.

So while cell-groups are at least an attempt at personal ministry, they are merely extentions of the church. The pastor is still head over all, and even though he doesn't know all the congregants on an intimately personal basis, he still rules over what they will hear and experience in their cell groups.

So the house assembly is not the cell-church movement that operates from within large congregations; rather, it is autonomous, largely unstructured, and independent from other fellowships, although there are (or will be) cooperative elements among them.

Neither is this a "restoration of the Church," as many cults claim to be. Nor is it a "Second Reformation," as some claim to be leading. Rather, it is merely the true believers separating themselves from the false brethren, the false apostles and the false teachers as the days of the end approach. And they will have no central authority other than Jesus Christ.

In short, the model of the first-century assemblies, devoid of a professional clergy class, dependent upon Scripture and the Holy Spirit to guide a plurality of leadership among godly men, is in the process of rebirth.

But, again, just because some people have separated themselves from the umbilical cord of the professional pastor does not mean they are offering any truth or purity of ministry. The form and function of the assembly is extremely important. In this book we merely offer guidelines that will hopefully aid those who are seeking a more biblical approach to gathering together than they have experienced within the institutional churches.

LOVE

In all aspects of gathering together in obedience to the Word of God (Hebrews 10:25), the primary element that must guide all teaching and practice is love. Even the forms and functions set forth herein are not to take precedence over the ministry in love by all within the assembly. Scripture relates how love takes precedence even over the Law of God:

> *And it came to pass, that he went through the corn fields on the sabbath day; and his disciples began, as they went, to pluck the ears of corn.*
>
> *And the Pharisees said unto him, Behold, why do they on the sabbath day that which is not lawful?*
>
> *And he said unto them, Have ye never read what David did, when he had need, and was an hungred, he, and they that were with him?*
>
> *How he went into the house of God in the days of Abiathar the high priest, and did eat the shewbread, which is not lawful to eat but for the priests, and gave also to them which were with him?*
>
> *And he said unto them, The sabbath was made for man, and not man for the sabbath:*
>
> *Therefore the Son of man is Lord also of the sabbath.* (Mark 2:23-28)

The Lord did not tell the Pharisees that they were wrong about keeping the Sabbath, but that they misunderstood the intent of the Law, which was for the benefit of man, given from the heart of a loving God. This must be kept in mind regarding all the forms and functions found even in Scripture as they relate to the assembling of believers.

As we look at the form and function of a biblical gathering we will contrast some of them with what is found in the institutional churches. This is not to cast aspersions upon the few godly men who are pastoring some of the churches, but to demonstrate how even the best are not functioning fully in accordance with God's Word.

3
The House Model

The establishment churches gather for the most part in buildings constructed for that purpose; some rent space in commercial buildings. Some meet in homes, but this does not automatically qualify them as the true *ekklesia* of God. As long as they adhere to the clergy-laity structure, they are not functioning fully as the Lord intended for His *ekklesia*.

House assemblies meet in the homes of those who gather together regularly. Is there something inherently wrong with meeting in a commercial building? Not on the face of it. It is not where the gathering takes place that counts as much as what goes on within the gathering. We could all meet on a lawn somewhere and it would still be honorable to God. However, there are serious drawbacks to institutional buildings.

One drawback is the cost for construction and maintenance, which depletes the store of funds available for meeting the needs of others. Another is the impersonal atmosphere that such buildings create, especially where the pews are arranged so that each person ends up staring at the back of someone's head. This fosters a clergy-laity mentality of the people and their leaders. The purpose of the church building has always been to create an identity of the institution as "the Church" rather than the people as the Body of Christ. The first church buildings were pagan temples converted to Catholic churches so that Constantine could help his Roman subjects more easily convert to Christianity. This compromise extended not only to the buildings, but to the activities held in the buildings.

Ever since then the church building has been used primarily as a forum for the pastor's pulpit messages, and for other purposes the pastor deems suitable. The use of church buildings generally revolves around the pastor's perceived ministry, not around the ministry of the brethren as a whole to one another. Thus, the less formal the setting, the better the atmosphere for all believers who are considered priests by God to be able to minister the gifts of the Spirit as God directs them.

Sadly, some who insist upon leaving the formality of the church building and the establishment religious setting desire merely to transfer the same form of religion into the house assembly. Many pastors begin by gathering people to their teaching in homes, only to expand to a church building later. Even some who do not wish to have a church building still use a pulpit forum where a single pastor is preeminent. They seem to think that because they meet in a house instead of a church building they are being more scriptural. All they are really doing is bolstering the pastor's ego at the expense of the brethren. Thus, they are not really escaping the institutional church setting.

For those who truly desire to escape the church setting, the best place to meet is in the homes of the brethren at large. This fits the pattern of the first-century assemblies:

> *And they, continuing daily with one accord in the temple, and breaking bread from house to house, did eat their meat with gladness and singleness of heart,*
> *Praising God, and having favour with all the people. And the Lord added to the assembly daily such as should be saved.* (Acts 2:46-47)

The establishment churches ignore the "house-to-house" portion and equate their buildings with the temple. The temple at Jerusalem no longer exists; we are the temple of the living God. The church buildings do not take the place of the temple, as some might want us to believe. There was no temple outside of Jerusalem, and all recorded instances of gatherings for the

Lord's *ekklesia* elsewhere took place in the homes of the believers (Acts 5:42; 16:40; 1 Corinthians 1:11; 16:15-19).

Some argue that the first-century believers also met in the Synagogues. True, but they did not meet as the *ekklesia* of Christ. They met to bring the Gospel to the yet unbelieving Jews. Eventually they were cast out of the synagogues which remained within the sphere of rabbinical Judaism. As the family of God they met in their homes (Acts 2:46; 5:42; 20:20; Romans 16:5; Philemon 1:2).

By meeting in the homes of the brethren at large, the assembly is not burdened with a financial obligation that would tie it to any particular building. If an elder apostatizes he may be summarily removed from the assembly; he is not the established resident of the "church building," often ensconced by some hierarchical system. Since the people other than the individual owners of the homes have no financial stake in the building where they meet, they will never be disenfranchised from any "investment." If they leave, they haven't lost thousands of dollars to the church that betrayed their trust.

WHEN TO MEET

Just as there are disputes in the establishment churches, there are disputes among those in the house assembly movement as to when the brethren should meet. Some insist that it must be on Sunday because they believe the Roman Catholic error that Sunday is "the Lord's Day" commemorating the alleged day Jesus rose from the dead. (For the truth about when Jesus actually rose see Media Spotlight's *Facts and Fallacies of the Resurrection: Did Jesus Really Die on Friday and Rise on Sunday?*)

Others are Sabbath keepers, and insist that the Sabbath was never changed by God, but by Roman Catholicism as a means to divorce "the Church" from its Jewish roots. They are correct in their assessment of the Roman Catholic influence, but they are mistaken in thinking that the Sabbath was instituted as a day of worship apart from all other days. Nowhere do the apostles command us to gather together on the Sabbath any more than on any other day.

Rabbinical Judaism established the custom of gathering in the synagogue (an invention of man, not God) on Sabbath. But this was not a command of God, who merely established the Sabbath as a day of rest from one's labors. The seventh-day Sabbath was also said to be a day of "holy convocation," but it is not clear if this was for the Sabbaths that occurred during the feasts, or for all seventh-day Sabbaths (Leviticus 23:1-36). If men chose to gather to worship or study Scripture on that day it was perfectly alright. After all, Jesus and His disciples met in the synagogues on Sabbath to proclaim the Gospel. But gathering together on the weekly Sabbath was never a command or even a suggestion for Jesus' disciples.

There are those who insist that the brethren must gather daily, citing Acts 2:46-47 and 5:42. But the situation in Jerusalem was unique; it was the beginning of Christ's *ekklesia* during a time of great persecution. Nothing else in Scripture states that this is a pattern that must be followed. It merely states what took place in a certain place at a certain time. Unlike the pattern established where the brethren met in houses in every instance, the idea of meeting every day is mentioned only of the brethren in Jerusalem at the very start.

So the question of when to meet should not even be an issue. The time to meet is when it is best for all or most of the brethren to gather on a regular basis. The day and time may even change on occasion. The idea that the brethren have to meet once a week (or two to seven times a week) at a given time in a given place robs the brethren of their freedom in Christ. The consensus of the assembly should determine the best times to meet as well as the best places to meet. There may be times when circumstances dictate meeting daily, or once a month, or any time between, perhaps even fewer than once a month if persecution prevents coming together more often. The important thing is that we not forsake gathering together; the more often we can do it the better.

HOW TO MEET

Churches like to set specific times and forms for meeting. This helps the pastor keep control and assures him that everyone will be there for his sermon, which is generally the concluding portion of the service. In the Lord's assemblies there should be no specific requirement for people to "attend" at a given time and remain until someone says, "go in peace." Many house assemblies conduct themselves in the same manner, and treat themselves as some sacred gathering to which everyone must adhere according to rules set forth by the leadership. There is no such mandate in Scripture. While we are all exhorted to not forget to gather together, who says we have to be there at a certain time and leave only when given permission to do so?

The Lord's assemblies should not have such constraints. Gatherings may last anywhere from four to eight hours or more, depending upon how things go. Those in the churches who are bored to tears waiting for the pastor to finish sermonizing might cringe at the thought of such a long period for gathering. But where God's Spirit is operative there is no boredom. In the process of such a meeting, however, there may be found the need for someone to leave before everything is concluded because they have a long journey home or must rise early the next morning for some reason such as going to work.

We do not judge or question why people decide to leave when they do. Nor do we judge or question why they arrive when they do. Those who take offense at others who do not "toe the line," are prideful, being offended that they are not "respected"—particularly those who might be sermonizing.

This does not mean that the brethren should be careless about their attendance. On the contrary, we should all respect the times designated for ministry. This demonstrates love for those who give of themselves for our spiritual benefit. But if circumstances compel us to be late to arrive or early to leave we should not be judged for it.

As we discuss the function of the assembly the reader will realize more fully why this is so. And if you think such a long period of time (by church standards) for gathering together is unreasonable, please reserve judgment until you have read this book in its entirety to find out just what takes place in the assembly.

4
The Function of the Assembly

Believers are beginning to look anew at the function of their gatherings. While the present unscriptural functions of the churches have operated for centuries, they have largely proven inadequate (in some cases even dangerous) to the spiritual and temporal welfare of Christ's true Body. Therefore, it behooves us to consider the scriptural model that will be necessary to adopt if believers are to be fruitful in the last days.

Jesus warns us of the persecution that will come not only from government, but from our own households and from the churches themselves:

> *Think not that I am come to send peace on earth: I came not to send peace, but a sword.*
>
> *For I am come to set a man at variance against his father, and the daughter against her mother, and the daughter in law against her mother in law.*
>
> *And a man's foes shall be they of his own household.* (Matthew 10:34-36)
>
> *They shall put you out of the synagogues: yea, the time cometh, that whosoever killeth you will think that he doeth God service.*
>
> *And these things will they do unto you, because they have not known the Father, nor me.* (John 16:2-3)

This writing is intended as a guide in structuring a local fellowship for those who may wish to join with brethren of like mind. My reasons for offering it are three-fold:

- To aid those already in house assemblies to recognize the biblical pattern for gathering together;

- To provide help for those who cannot find a biblical fellowship in their area;

- To provide help for the days when the true believers will have to function in a closer-knit community for the sake of survival—days of persecution or societal breakdown.

The details are important, but more important is the bottom line, which is to gather with those of like mind and to love and care for one another. Allow the Holy Spirit to do what He will in your midst. You will recognize the elders among you, and you will give them place for authority in your lives as you function within the body of believers.

Yet we must not take a laissez-faire attitude if the assembly is to function as a legitimate expression of the Lord's Body. Therefore, it is my intent to offer some insight into the proper function of the assembly, and its accountability to God's Word for all doctrine and practice. Take what I offer and use what you can. Check the Scriptures to make sure your pattern conforms. While God grants some liberty in determining the form of ministry, there are also strict biblical guidelines in several areas pertaining to the form of ministry and to the function of members, from the eldest in leadership to the new convert.

It is my hope that this will clarify the biblical position and make distinctions between what Scripture requires and what church tradition has established.

I recognize that not everyone can receive what I write here. That's okay, and it doesn't diminish their position to disagree with me. But for those who can receive what is said, I believe they will enter into an experience that will both bless them and test their commitment to the Lord and to the Body of Christ.

Some things may be considered relatively unimportant in relation to other things. Certainly our freedom in Christ should allow for differences where Scripture does not speak clearly. But where Scripture does speak clearly we are bound to listen and apply what it says. In such cases, to exercise freedom would be to take license with the grace of God.

The question may arise as to who I am that the Lord would use me to bring this message and to address these issues. To this I can only answer, "Beats me." All I can say is that over the past 26 years that we have been publishing *Media Spotlight*, I've gained a lot of insight into the religious climate of the world. And, just as Paul says in 1 Corinthians 7:40, I can say, "I think also that I have the Spirit of God."

THE FUNCTION OF THE ASSEMBLY

The function of the assembly can be summed up in the following ministries:

- To teach Scripture;

- To hold accountable to Scripture;

- To expose and warn against false teachings and teachers;

- To evangelize the lost;

- To provide fellowship;

- To provide corporate worship;

- To pray for one another;

- To bear one another's burdens;

- To minister to those in need spiritually and temporally.

As we look at each of these ministries individually we learn that all are indispensible for the spiritual health of the local assembly. Yet for the most part they are not being implemented properly (some not at all) in many of today's churches. The Lord's people have been robbed of their inheritance by the very institutions that demand their allegiance and monetary support.

To Teach Scripture

Go ye therefore, and teach all nations, baptizing them in the name of the Father, and of the Son, and of the Holy Ghost:

Teaching them to observe all things whatsoever I have commanded you: and, lo, I am with you alway, even unto the end of the world. Amen. (Matthew 28:19-20)

The teaching ministry is to be in the hands of men who hold Scripture in the highest regard. It isn't enough to believe that God's Word is inerrant and wholly inspired by the Holy Spirit; a teacher of God's Word must avoid integrating with Scripture other theological philosophies based on human wisdom.

There are many who would agree that the Bible is inspired by the Holy Spirit and contains no error. But they would add that truth can be found in other philosophies outside of Scripture as well. This is because they have bought into the humanistic lie that "all truth is God's truth," and what may be true for one person may not be true for another person. This subjective approach to truth is more often the result of naïveté and ignorance than evil intent.

The argument is that there are scientific truths that are not contained in Scripture, and many day-to-day facts with which Scripture does not deal. No one would argue with that. But those who state this often use it as an excuse to incorporate into their teaching certain philosophical beliefs which are either unbiblical or extra-biblical. Because some theological truth may be found in beliefs apart from biblical faith, they assume that they may trust other things found in those philosophies.

Truth, as defined theologically, pertains to all that God has revealed for the spiritual and temporal benefit of man. Facts may pertain to certain things that exist in the temporal realm, and may or may not contribute to man's temporal benefit. An example of the latter would be detailed teaching on diet and exercise, science, mathematics, and other human disciplines. In some cases these may overlap onto what Scripture has to say about these subjects, but no genuine facts will ever contradict Scripture.

Failing to understand this fundamental difference between truth and fact, many pastors have strayed into areas of spiritual fornication, adopting for their beliefs teachings that are rooted in human wisdom and philosophy, some elements of which may find agreement with Scripture. The integration of psychological theory with biblical truth is one such practice which has become commonplace in many of today's churches. The reasoning is that Scripture gives broad guidelines to human behavior, but psychology provides in-depth, scientific insight into specific behavioral problems. By combining the two it is hoped that a more perfect understanding of human behavior and how to correct it may be had than if one were to rely upon Scripture alone.

But has this approach resulted in a discernible holiness that would rival that of the early believers? On the contrary, the churches have become more worldly. But what can be expected when they adopt the world's beliefs and practices as somehow equal to or better than those revealed in God's Word?

It remains that the only answer to sin is repentance and obedience to God's Word. The key is humility (self-abasement), not the building up of one's self-esteem (personal pride) as claimed by the psychological integrationists.

It is incumbent upon the teachers in the local assemblies to eschew human wisdom and philosophy, and to teach only God's Word. In other words, it is the elder's responsibility to teach God's Word; it is not their responsibility to teach anything other than God's Word.

This does not mean they may not address current events and topics that impact their members. It means they must avoid all philosophical teachings except to occasionally contrast them with Scripture for the purpose of defending the Faith. Teaching may also include things that pertain to godliness and practical matters that are of benefit to the believer, as long as those teachings do not contradict Scripture. Nor should they impair the teaching of Scripture by taking an inordinate amount of time designated for teaching. An occasional anecdote that relates to the scriptural teaching may be used, but such should be kept to a minimum.

The Manner of Teaching

For many churches the teaching ministry takes the following form:

- The pastor may or may not have the people open to a verse of Scripture;

- He reads the passage aloud;

- The Bible is closed and the pastor expounds for 30 to 45 minutes on the single verse or passage, interspersing anecdotes, humorous quips and interpretations gleaned from commentaries or professional sermon outlines. (In some cases he will reference other verses that bolster the message.);

- There is seldom any in-depth teaching or prophetic proclamation, and often the verse is taken out of context so that, rather than the literal meaning of God's Word, the meaning the pastor wants to convey is transmitted to the congregation.

God's Word is unique. It contains a life of its own. Were teachers to guide their listeners through verse-by-verse reading, pausing only to remark upon those verses that require special attention at the time, the people would become immersed in Scripture rather than in men's opinions of Scripture.

The rabbinical schools of Israel made a mistake that is being emulated by religious leaders today. They spent hours applying esoteric interpretations of Scripture that they had learned from other rabbis, debating fine points of the Law and establishing themselves, rather than the clear, open and life-giving Scriptures, as the authority.

In the same manner, people in many of today's churches do not hear God's Word proclaimed or taught as much as they hear the pastor's interpretation of God's Word. And the interpretations are often clouded by theological biases learned in Bible schools and seminaries.

Rabbinical Judaism builds synagogues in which they teach their traditions mingled with Scripture. Pastoral Christianity builds churches for the same purpose. Both largely make the Word of God of no effect through their traditions.

The churches have lost sight of the truth that the pastor is not the authority, Scripture is the authority. Only as biblically-qualified elders teach and lead according to the clear meaning of Scripture can they exercise legitimate authority in the fellowship.

Teaching vs. Preaching

Some elders prefer the teaching method to convey God's truths; others prefer the preaching method. What's the difference, and which is more important?

A sound teacher will focus on the text, expounding on the meanings of words, the context of the narrative, and the specific message of the Scriptures in question.

Preaching is a form of teaching that focuses attention on a specific message and integrates the applicable texts to bolster that message. Sometimes more than one message will be conveyed.

Both methods of handling God's Word are valid as long as the integrity of the Scriptures and their meaning are maintained. The problem lies in focusing on one form of addressing the assembly to the exclusion (or near exclusion) of the other form.

Preaching is a form of prophetic ministry. The elder gifted with the prophetic ministry has his hand upon the pulse of the assembly. He is sensitive to the strengths and weaknesses of the people, not so much due to "inspiration," but due to discernment based upon knowledge. He is emboldened to exhort the brethren to holy living, applying God's Word to his exhortation. Ideally, every elder should be able to both teach and preach as the Holy Spirit leads.

To Hold Accountable To Scripture

Obey them that have the rule over you, and submit yourselves: for they watch for your souls, as they that must give account, that they may do it with joy, and not with grief: for that is unprofitable for you. (Hebrews 13:17)

It is one thing to teach God's Word; it is another thing to hold the people accountable to what has been taught. Elders have no business holding the brethren accountable to anything other than the clear teachings of the Bible. The reason for the scandals that plagued the shepherding movement was that the false "shepherds" were intruding into areas of personal living that were outside their rightful domain. They took on far more than is allowed by God's Word.

Unfaithful shepherds will either abuse the flock by demanding obedience to dictates not found in God's Word, or will neglect the flock by not holding them strictly to the demands of God's Word. Either way, they are failing those whom they have taken under their care.

The proper approach to accountability will provide a loving but firm hand upon those entrusted to the assembly's leadership. The process will include —both corporately and individually—instruction in righteousness according to Scripture. It will include encouragement to remain faithful to God's Word, exhortation to take a stand for God's Word, and reproof and rebuke for not adhering to God's Word. It will also include necessary discipline as a consequence for not obeying God's Word. Finally, it will require exposure and even disfellowshipping of those who rebel against correction meant to bring them into conformity to God's Word.

Those who refuse correction after one or two admonitions are to be removed from the fellowship (Titus 3:10). This doesn't leave much room for bearing with rebellion. But leadership must be sure that the thing to which they are demanding obedience is clearly stated in God's Word, and is not based upon tradition or theological biases.

It is extremely important, however, to stress that genuine love and concern for a brother's soul must be the basis for all discipline. Let those who would impose such discipline examine themselves first to see if they are not condemning a brother for their own sins.

To Warn Against False Teachings And Teachers

For I know this, that after my departing shall grievous wolves enter in among you, not sparing the flock.

Also of your own selves shall men arise, speaking perverse things, to draw away disciples after them.

Therefore watch, and remember, that by the space of three years I ceased not to warn every one night and day with tears. (Acts 20:29-31)

Many Christians are critical of those who expend time and effort to expose false teachings, especially inside the churches. They insist that we are to only proclaim the Gospel and not judge others; the Holy Spirit will do that. But if this were true, false teachings would not proliferate as they have throughout the centuries. The hierarchical system that characterizes most churches would not exist today; cults would not so easily spring up to lure people away from the truth.

To hold to the position that leaders are to only proclaim the Gospel and not expose error contrary to the Gospel is to fail to proclaim the whole Gospel. It looks at the Gospel as only conveying the message of salvation through the blood of Christ, without regard to the rest of Scripture's instructions. In effect, it births souls into the Kingdom of God, but doesn't nurture them or protect them from danger, which any good parent would do for their child. What good parent would give birth, and then leave it up to God to take care of their child's welfare, refusing to feed it, clothe it, or instruct it on the dangers of life?

Yet that is what many pastors do with those under their care. They avoid the controversy of confronting spiritual error, and do not employ scriptural discipline for fear of losing members. This is cowardice.

If there were ever a time in history that believers must be warned against false teachings and false teachers, this is that time. It is in keeping with scriptural prophecy that as we approach the end of this age evil will increase and false prophets will proliferate:

> *And as he sat upon the mount of Olives, the disciples came unto him privately, saying, Tell us, when shall these things be? and what shall be the sign of thy coming, and of the end of the world?*
>
> *And Jesus answered and said unto them, Take heed that no man deceive you.*
>
> *For many shall come in my name, saying, I am Christ; and shall deceive many.*
>
> *And ye shall hear of wars and rumours of wars: see that ye be not troubled: for all these things must come to pass, but the end is not yet.*
>
> *For nation shall rise against nation, and kingdom against kingdom: and there shall be famines, and pestilences, and earthquakes, in divers places.*
>
> *All these are the beginning of sorrows.*
>
> *Then shall they deliver you up to be afflicted, and shall kill you: and ye shall be hated of all nations for my name's sake.*
>
> *And then shall many be offended, and shall betray one another, and shall hate one another.*
>
> *And many false prophets shall rise, and shall deceive many.*
>
> *And because iniquity shall abound, the love of many shall wax cold.*
>
> *But he that shall endure unto the end, the same shall be saved.* (Matthew 24:3-13)

Almost all of the biblical writers warned of deception and urged the brethren to put up their guards. Defense of the Faith is as important to spiritual life as is defense against wolves to the shepherd guarding his flock. It is important that everyone with

knowledge of error—especially the shepherds of God's flock—
warn the people against that error and earnestly contend for the
Faith (Jude 3). Paul was adamant about this:

> *Now I beseech you, brethren, mark them which
> cause divisions and offences contrary to the doctrine
> which ye have learned; and avoid them.*
>
> *For they that are such serve not our Lord Jesus
> Christ, but their own belly; and by good words and
> fair speeches deceive the hearts of the simple. (Romans
> 16:17-18)*

Paul is telling us divisions are caused by false doctrine. It is
not those who defend the truth that cause division, but those
who introduce error. *They* must bear the blame for dividing the
Body of Christ. We must hold fast to truth:

> *That we henceforth be no more children, tossed to
> and fro, and carried about with every wind of doctrine,
> by the sleight of men, and cunning craftiness, whereby
> they lie in wait to deceive;*
>
> *But speaking the truth in love, may grow up into
> him in all things, which is the head, even Christ:*
> (Ephesians 4:14-15)
>
> *Knowing this, that the law is not made for a
> righteous man, but for the lawless and disobedient, for
> the ungodly and for sinners, for unholy and profane,
> for murderers of fathers and murderers of mothers, for
> manslayers,*
>
> *For whoremongers, for them that defile themselves
> with mankind, for menstealers, for liars, for perjured
> persons, and if there be any other thing that is contrary
> to sound doctrine;*
>
> *According to the glorious gospel of the blessed God,
> which was committed to my trust.* (1 Timothy 1:9-11)

We often categorize sins according to how we perceive
their relative evil. Yet Scripture places among these despicable

sins "any other thing that is contrary to sound doctrine." If men will preach against other evils, why not against false doctrine?

> *If thou put the brethren in remembrance of these things, thou shalt be a good minister of Jesus Christ, nourished up in the words of faith and of good doctrine, whereunto thou hast attained.*
>
> *But refuse profane and old wives' fables, and exercise thyself rather unto godliness.* (1 Timothy 4:6-7)
>
> *Till I come, give attendance to reading, to exhortation, to doctrine.* (1 Timothy 4:13)
>
> *Take heed unto thyself, and unto the doctrine; continue in them: for in doing this thou shalt both save thyself, and them that hear thee.* (1 Timothy 4:16)
>
> *If any man teach otherwise, and consent not to wholesome words, even the words of our Lord Jesus Christ, and to the doctrine which is according to godliness;*
>
> *He is proud, knowing nothing, but doting about questions and strifes of words, whereof cometh envy, strife, railings, evil surmisings,*
>
> *Perverse disputings of men of corrupt minds, and destitute of the truth, supposing that gain is godliness: from such withdraw thyself.* (1 Timothy 6:3-5)
>
> *Preach the word; be instant in season, out of season; reprove, rebuke, exhort with all longsuffering and doctrine.*
>
> *For the time will come when they will not endure sound doctrine; but after their own lusts shall they heap to themselves teachers, having itching ears;*
>
> *And they shall turn away their ears from the truth, and shall be turned unto fables.* (2 Timothy 4:2-4)

Paul names the proclaiming of sound doctrine as a duty of the elders:

Holding fast the faithful word as he hath been taught, that he may be able by sound doctrine both to exhort and to convince the gainsayers. (Titus 1:9)

Sound doctrine goes beyond the rudiments of the Gospel, even to sanctification, or separation from sin—the teaching of how believers should conduct themselves:

But speak thou the things which become sound doctrine:

That the aged men be sober, grave, temperate, sound in faith, in charity, in patience.

The aged women likewise, that they be in behaviour as becometh holiness, not false accusers, not given to much wine, teachers of good things;

That they may teach the young women to be sober, to love their husbands, to love their children,

To be discreet, chaste, keepers at home, good, obedient to their own husbands, that the word of God be not blasphemed.

Young men likewise exhort to be sober minded.

In all things shewing thyself a pattern of good works: in doctrine shewing uncorruptness, gravity, sincerity,

Sound speech, that cannot be condemned; that he that is of the contrary part may be ashamed, having no evil thing to say of you.

Exhort servants to be obedient unto their own masters, and to please them well in all things; not answering again;

Not purloining, but shewing all good fidelity; that they may adorn the doctrine of God our Saviour in all things.

For the grace of God that bringeth salvation hath appeared to all men,

Teaching us that, denying ungodliness and worldly lusts, we should live soberly, righteously, and godly, in this present world;

Looking for that blessed hope, and the glorious appearing of the great God and our Saviour Jesus Christ;

Who gave himself for us, that he might redeem us from all iniquity, and purify unto himself a peculiar people, zealous of good works.

These things speak, and exhort, and rebuke with all authority. Let no man despise thee. (Titus 2:1-15)

Read these Scriptures carefully, and you will see why many pastors don't want to think of them as necessary for adherence to sound doctrine. They would incur the wrath of many women (and men) for daring to suggest these things are necessary to the Faith.

These and other Scriptures have much to say about teaching and adhering to sound doctrine. But this is only possible if sound doctrine is contrasted with false doctrine, much of which sounds scriptural to the unlearned. This, without a doubt, would require that pastors study hard to keep up with the winds of doctrine that are affecting their charges through the Christian media and elsewhere. They must know what the enemy is saying so they can counter the error with sound doctrine. Naïveté and ignorance do not excuse those whose life work is serving God's people.

However, each of us must go beyond examining ourselves to see if we are in the Faith; we must also examine those with whom we fellowship, and especially those who teach us. We must examine our leaders by the light of God's Word, and test what they teach and encourage us to practice. As perils increase it will become all the more imperative that we know whom we can trust, especially among leadership.

Are our leaders warning us of deceptions in our midst, or are they content to leave those things alone, fearing that they may lose a good number of their adherants? Or are they encouraging us to get involved in questionable movements, overlooking serious error for the sake of an emotional experience?

Are they preparing us for a worst-case scenario should the Lord not remove us from tribulation as many are hoping for?

These and many other questions must be asked if we are to continue to trust those who oversee our spiritual welfare. Time is too short to continue playing church; if we are not serious about sacrificing all we have for the Lord and for service to His people, we are not ready to meet Him.

In His parable about the Kingdom of Heaven (Matthew 25:14-30), Jesus delineated between the profitable servant and the lazy servant. His closing words are sobering:

> *For unto every one that hath shall be given, and he shall have abundance: but from him that hath not shall be taken away even that which he hath.*
>
> *And cast ye the unprofitable servant into outer darkness: there shall be weeping and gnashing of teeth.* (Matthew 25:29-30)

May we all be counted as profitable servants, occupying and working in the vineyard of the Lord when He returns.

To Evangelize The Lost
But watch thou in all things, endure afflictions, do the work of an evangelist, make full proof of thy ministry. (2 Timothy 4:5)

All believers are called to be witnesses and to evangelize the lost, and there are those gifted with evangelistic fervor who may or may not bear the gift of evangelism.

There is a place for mass evangelism as evidenced by Scripture (Acts 2:41; 4:4). But during times of persecution mass evangelism may not be practical.

One-on-one evangelism is still the mainstay of the Gospel. Our personal witness carries much weight when combined with God's Word.

Yet every fellowship should have an evangelist among the eldership. The evangelist primarily concerns himself with the lost who are brought into the fellowship to be witnessed to.

This does not mean that the evangelist may not also function in other gifts. But it is primarily he who should confront the unbeliever and offer him an opportunity to surrender his life to Christ. This is a gift often neglected in the modern churches where confrontation is avoided at all costs. In most churches evangelism is limited to missionary work outside the fellowship—often in foreign countries—which more often than not take the forms of temporal aid and entertainment rather than the literal proclaiming of the Gospel.

Missionary work, though often entered into by selfless people who truly desire to see the lost saved, does not meet the immediate need to present the Gospel to unbelievers who come into the midst of the assembly. In the churches this need is usually met with an appeal from the pulpit (by pastors who usurp the gift of evangelist) to "come to Jesus" so He can alleviate their troubles. And while our Father, because of our faith in His Son, Jesus, does often alleviate our troubles, that is an erroneous premise upon which to base the Gospel message. Bringing someone to church in the hope that something said from the pulpit will cause them to "accept Christ" is, at best, a weak attempt at evangelism. It exposes the unbeliever to a generic gospel that may or may not convict him of sin and lead him to repentance. It is important that people be made aware of their sinful nature and their inability to please God with their works apart from faith in Jesus Christ.

As well, most appeals in the churches to "accept Christ" focus on the benefits of salvation without mention of the consequences of following Christ: tribulations, rejection by friends and family, loss of jobs, ridicule by former associates with whom they had engaged in sinful activities, persecution and possible torture and death for the sake of the Gospel.

There are those who believe that counting the cost must come after one is convinced to follow the Lord due to the preaching of his need for Christ. After he makes the commitment he must be told to count the cost. This is dishonest and places more emphasis upon "closing the sale," than on making sound converts.

Then there are those who never even address the issue.

Others believe that the non-believer must first be convinced of his need to surrender to Christ, but before he is encouraged to make a commitment he should be told of the consequences.

This latter position is the correct one. It is based on the belief that the former position might cause one to violate his stated commitment, which could bring a greater judgment upon him. In either case, Jesus Himself tells us to count the cost before choosing to follow Him:

> *If any man come to me, and hate not his father, and mother, and wife, and children, and brethren, and sisters, yea, and his own life also, he cannot be my disciple.*
>
> *And whosoever doth not bear his cross, and come after me, cannot be my disciple.*
>
> *For which of you, intending to build a tower, sitteth not down first, and counteth the cost, whether he have sufficient to finish it?*
>
> *Lest haply, after he hath laid the foundation, and is not able to finish it, all that behold it begin to mock him,*
>
> *Saying, This man began to build, and was not able to finish.*
>
> *Or what king, going to make war against another king, sitteth not down first, and consulteth whether he be able with ten thousand to meet him that cometh against him with twenty thousand?*
>
> *Or else, while the other is yet a great way off, he sendeth an ambassage, and desireth conditions of peace.*
>
> *So likewise, whosoever he be of you that forsaketh not all that he hath, he cannot be my disciple.*
>
> *Salt is good: but if the salt have lost his savour, wherewith shall it be seasoned?*
>
> *It is neither fit for the land, nor yet for the dunghill; but men cast it out. He that hath ears to hear, let him hear.* (Luke 15:25-35)

Jesus never made it easy to follow Him— certainly not as easy as those who preach today's incomplete gospel appear to make it.

To ignore the consequences of following Christ as a disciple—not merely as a "Christian"—is to defraud the listener. What lies behind the watered-down gospel is a fear of rejection and a desire to just "get them in the door" and let the Holy Spirit take it from there.

By God's mercy, some do enter that way and eventually become strong disciples of the Lord. But that does not negate the cowardice of the preacher or absolve him of responsibility for failing to present the true Gospel in its entirety.

People new to the assembly must be asked by the elders what they believe and why they believe it. They must be given time to prove their faithfulness to Christ and to the brethren before being placed in positions of responsibility or asked to minister. Too often new people are placed into positions of leadership based on perceived "spiritual gifts." In reality, they are being promoted in the assembly because of their expertise in displaying their natural talents. In some churches personality tests are mandated for those who desire a ministry in order for the pastor to know where to pigeon-hole them.

If the people are truly humble and possess the other characteristics of the fruit of the Spirit they will submit to the requirement of testing their faith, not some psychological test, before being allowed to hold any position of service in the assembly. If they do not wish to submit to that test, or if they insist they must be believed qualified to minister based upon their outward piety, they are, in fact, not qualified and must be instructed of that truth.

The Open Door Policy

Most churches operate on an "open door policy," publicly inviting everyone to join them in their services. The idea is to reach the unchurched and increase the membership roles. This policy is acceptable for evangelistic ministry and for the synagogue or teaching center, which most of today's churches are. But it reflects an improper understanding of the assembly's primary purpose.

The assembly is the family of God. It is meant to be a closed community wherein the brethren gather to share the common Faith. To open its doors to all comers invites a weakening of the family structure. It places more importance upon unbelievers who think they are Christians than it does upon the family of God itself. For the underground assembly it could be dangerous.

All sorts of ungodly elements come into the churches. This results in corruption of the body of believers. Transients are not held accountable for the errors they introduce among the brethren, or for their personal sins which remain secret for lack of familiarity between them and the elders. As a result, God's people are found worshipping Him in the company of heathens.

By transients I am not referring only to those who visit on occasion; many long-standing members of churches are transients in that they do not submit to any spiritual authority, or do not wish to be active participants within the body of believers. Nor are the leaders in an open-door-policy church inclined to hold the people accountable. But, then, how can they if they don't know the people?

This does not mean that a totally closed-door policy should be followed. It merely means that, ideally, anyone outside the body who would come into the assembly should be brought by invitation of a member of that assembly. If the person is unsaved, the purpose must be to expose that person to the Gospel on a personal level, ministered by those qualified to relate the Gospel and explain the consequences of turning to Christ for salvation. Any open-door policy should be according to the discretion of the elders as they see the purpose and consider the consequences of that policy.

Because of today's easy-believism preached from corrupt pulpits, and the haste to promote people, the churches are filled with backsliders, malcontents, rebellious, argumentative and disrespectful wives and children, and sin of every sort.

Because the pure Word of God has been blended with human wisdom, holiness and fear toward God are lacking. And without fear of God, wisdom is lacking (Psalm 111:10).

Because wisdom is lacking, the people are falling into snares, and spiritual death is raising a stench in the nostrils of God (Proverbs 10:21).

In every *good* sense, the Body of Christ is to be a cult—separated from the world's evils while at the same time living in the world as salt and light. But if the salt has lost its savor. . . .

To Provide Fellowship

And let us consider one another to provoke unto love and to good works:
Not forsaking the assembling of ourselves together, as the manner of some is; but exhorting one another: and so much the more, as ye see the day approaching. (Hebrews 10:24-25)

Strength is found in numbers. The Lord knows our need to be among those of like mind in the Faith. For the most part the believer's time is spent in the world, being bombarded by sensual appeals to his fleshly appetites. Even normal day-to-day activities take their toll. It is imperative that we receive strength from one another so that we may be able to stand in the day of trial and temptation. In fact, almost every day is a day of trial and temptation, often bringing sorrow and/or pain in some form.

Fellowship in the Body of Christ allows for the bearing of one another's burdens; it allows for opportunities to have doubts quelled, questions answered, and godly fellowship built.

If we are in constant close fellowship with the saints we are less likely to succumb to temptations; our conscience will not allow for godly conversation in the midst of personal guilt, and we will not want that conflict to exist. The presence of godly people helps godly people. Fellowship with ungodly people will corrupt (1 Corinthians 15:33).

It is not enough to fellowship for a few hours during and after a church service. Fellowship must be engaged in on a consistent basis. The first-century believers gathered daily in different homes to hear the Word of God, and to fellowship with one another.

Their custom of combining the gathering for worship, praise and teaching, along with a corporate meal and hours of fellowship on the Sabbath (and even daily), was replaced by ecclesiastical services which relied upon clerics for intercession and all participation. Eventually choirs took the place of spontaneous contribution of song by the congregants. The mass took the place of the community meal, and the priests' sermons took the place of preaching and teaching by the elders.

Protestantism shook off the priesthood by name, but retained the clergy-laity concept. The people were allowed to sing, but only at the behest of sanctioned worship leaders and often only in concert with the choir. The communion, while not the idolatrous ritual of Roman Catholicism, is still administered by the pastor who blesses the bread and the cup. The corporate meal is seldom found in most churches except on special occasions such as holiday celebrations.

Ideally, the gathering should have no time constraints. Everyone should be encouraged to contribute, provided they are known to be true believers of good report. This would alleviate the stranger-to-stranger casual contact most churches generate by their impersonal clergy-laity atmosphere.

But what about the megachurches? These require more than one service; there must be time constraints to allow for each service to remain on schedule.

Remember, we are addressing the conditions for the first-century assembly model. If a church is too big to do things properly then it's too big, period. Better that it divide itself into more autonomous, local assemblies that allow for more participation.

Were the gathering held over a period of hours, people could come and go as their needs required, or as the Lord allowed under difficult circumstances. The meal could be planned for a certain time to allow for convenience, as could some of the teaching and some of the worship, but all else, including additional teaching and worship, should be relatively spontaneous. That additional teaching, preaching, prayer, praise, worship and ministry could be engaged in throughout the day.

In this way the family of God would be just that—a family in the true sense of the word. Unbelievers who are brought by members would marvel at the love and close fellowship. They would know we are disciples of Jesus by our love for one another. As it is, they are brought to sterile proceedings conducted under formal auspices and polite non-committal greetings. Even the most "alive" churches fail to provide all the ministry God has ordained for His assembly. Formality and politeness should not be confused with reverence and consideration. If all things are to be done decently and in order (1 Corinthians 14:40), then reverence toward God and consideration of one another is imperative. Formality is for strangers, not for family.

The application of reverence and consideration still allow for spontaneous and full involvement by the whole family of God. In today's transient society this is extremely difficult. Many desire such fellowship, but there are few others of like mind—those who insist on purity of doctrine and practice—to provide for it. So we do the best we can by keeping our associations primarily among the brethren, on as consistent a basis as we can.

Some may argue in favor of the forms they are used to, and if that's what they want they can stay in their church. What I offer here is meant to cause thought on how the body of believers may better honor God and allow participation by all who feel led by the Spirit to praise Him at any given time, provided all is done in order and nothing is done to interrupt what is taking place at the moment. If someone is praying, prophesying, teaching or preaching, they should not be interrupted by someone who feels "moved" to take the lead. This is the consideration aspect of fellowship.

To Provide Corporate Worship

Let the word of Christ dwell in you richly in all wisdom; teaching and admonishing one another in psalms and hymns and spiritual songs, singing with grace in your hearts to the Lord. (Colossians 3:16)

We all have a need to worship our Creator. While this may be accomplished on the individual level, there is something uniquely edifying in corporate worship. The infectious atmosphere of group praise results in a heightened sense of belonging to the family of God. This has a beneficial effect upon our spiritual walk.

Scripture indicates that spontaneous praise in word and song, led by the prompting of the Holy Spirit, should be the norm (Ephesians 5:19; Colossians 3:16). Music to God's ears is not always the same as music to our ears. We listen to the sounds while He hears the heart sing.

Now, not just any sound is acceptable for worship and praise. The maintaining of reverence, even while making a "joyful noise" is important. (See Appendix B - "Music.") If anyone does get out of hand, it is up to the elders to maintain control so that all things are done decently and in order (1 Corinthians 14:40).

Whatever form the worship takes, those leading should consider whether it appeals to the soul or to the spirit. We often mistake good feelings for spirituality when, in fact, they may be carnal. This doesn't mean that when we are truly fed spiritually it doesn't produce good feelings. But the criterion that should guide us is that the worship causes us to focus on the object of our worship rather than on the feelings themselves.

This is often a fine line, but we should be on safe ground if we keep all things within the scope of reverence and sobriety, notwithstanding that our worship certainly may also be joyous as opposed to "happy."

To Pray For One Another

For this cause we also, since the day we heard it, do not cease to pray for you, and to desire that ye might be filled with the knowledge of his will in all wisdom and spiritual understanding. (Colossians 1:9)

Prayer is one aspect of ministry that can be—indeed must be—entered into by all members of the Body. Intercession is important to our realization of other's needs, and to the demonstration of love for them.

There are no qualifications for prayer other than that we live our lives in such a way that our prayers are not hindered. This is illustrated in Peter's exhortation to husbands to honor their wives as weaker vessels, yet equal in their relationship to God:

> *Likewise, ye husbands, dwell with them according to knowledge, giving honour unto the wife, as unto the weaker vessel, and as being heirs together of the grace of life; that your prayers be not hindered.* (1 Peter 3:7)

This instruction, however, does not apply only to the husband-wife relationship, but to every relationship with man and with God. This verse is found within several whose context is exhortation to godly living:

> *Likewise, ye wives, be in subjection to your own husbands; that, if any obey not the word, they also may without the word be won by the conversation of the wives;*
>
> *While they behold your chaste conversation coupled with fear.*
>
> *Whose adorning let it not be that outward adorning of plaiting the hair, and of wearing of gold, or of putting on of apparel;*
>
> *But let it be the hidden man of the heart, in that which is not corruptible, even the ornament of a meek and quiet spirit, which is in the sight of God of great price.*
>
> *For after this manner in the old time the holy women also, who trusted in God, adorned themselves, being in subjection unto their own husbands:*
>
> *Even as Sara obeyed Abraham, calling him lord: whose daughters ye are, as long as ye do well, and are not afraid with any amazement.*
>
> *Likewise, ye husbands, dwell with them according to knowledge, giving honour unto the wife, as unto the weaker vessel, and as being heirs together of the grace of life that your prayers be not hindered.*
>
> *Finally, be ye all of one mind, having compassion one of another, love as brethren, be pitiful, be courteous:*

Not rendering evil for evil, or railing for railing: but contrariwise blessing; knowing that ye are thereunto called, that ye should inherit a blessing.

For he that will love life, and see good days, let him refrain his tongue from evil, and his lips that they speak no guile:

Let him eschew evil, and do good; let him seek peace, and ensue it.

For the eyes of the Lord are over the righteous, and his ears are open unto their prayers: but the face of the Lord is against them that do evil. (1 Peter 3:1-12)

A woman who is not in subjection to her husband should have no more confidence in answered prayer than a husband who does not love and honor his wife. Nor, for that matter, should anyone who is not being obedient or walking in the love of God toward all men:

I exhort therefore, that, first of all, supplications, prayers, intercessions, and giving of thanks, be made for all men;

For kings, and for all that are in authority; that we may lead a quiet and peaceable life in all godliness and honesty.

For this is good and acceptable in the sight of God our Saviour;

Who will have all men to be saved, and to come unto the knowledge of the truth. (1 Timothy 2:1-4)

The requirement for prayer is that we live righteously before God and men. This righteousness is not a false piety, but a humble attitude that submits to the commandments of the Lord as stated in Scripture. At the heart of all of the Lord's commandments is the command to love not only those who love us, but those who hate us and persecute us. And if we truly love God we will keep His commandments:

Verily, verily, I say unto you, He that believeth on me, the works that I do shall he do also; and greater works than these shall he do; because I go unto my Father.

And whatsoever ye shall ask in my name, that will I do, that the Father may be glorified in the Son.

If ye shall ask any thing in my name, I will do it.

If ye love me, keep my commandments. (John 14:12-15)

So often people want to focus on verse 14, "If ye shall ask any thing in my name, I will do it," without regard to verse 15, "If ye love me, keep my commandments." They insist that they need not be too concerned about living righteously because Christ is their righteousness; as long as they believe in Jesus, it doesn't really matter how they conduct their lives; their only loss will be rewards, not salvation. This is a deception that treats God's grace and His rewards for faithfulness with contempt. It also hinders one's prayers from being answered. If how we live our lives is of little or no importance, why is Scripture filled with admonitions to conduct ourselves according to godliness? And how can love be genuine if we esteem our own desires above those of God?

When Jesus promised that where two or more are gathered in His name He would be in their midst (Matthew 18:20), He was speaking primarily within the context of ministry within the assembly. At the center of that ministry must lie sacrificial love for the brethren and for the Lord. For it is where true love in the Spirit dwells that the Lord manifests Himself:

He that hath my commandments, and keepeth them, he it is that loveth me: and he that loveth me shall be loved of my Father, and I will love him, and will manifest myself to him.

Judas saith unto him, not Iscariot, Lord, how is it that thou wilt manifest thyself unto us, and not unto the world?

Jesus answered and said unto him, If a man love me, he will keep my words: and my Father will love him, and we will come unto him, and make our abode with him.

He that loveth me not keepeth not my sayings: and the word which ye hear is not mine, but the Father's which sent me. (John 14:21-24)

To think that any two or three Christians can just get together and pray and the Lord will have to answer is to miss the point of this promise. Unless love for God's commandments is manifested in the believers who are gathered, the Lord is not in their midst.

Love for God and for man forms the basis for all righteousness in our thoughts and practices. And, again, while we are justified by faith, and not by the deeds of the law, we cannot willfully (holding a rebellious attitude without repentance) disobey God's commandments and still be saved. This is why James wrote that faith without works is dead, being alone (James 2:26). The evidence of our faith is our obedience to God.

The evidence of our obedience to God is our adherence to the commandment to love one another in the manner prescribed by Scripture:

Let love be without dissimulation. Abhor that which is evil; cleave to that which is good.

Be kindly affectioned one to another with brotherly love; in honour preferring one another;

Not slothful in business; fervent in spirit; serving the Lord;

Rejoicing in hope; patient in tribulation; continuing instant in prayer;

Distributing to the necessity of saints; given to hospitality.

Bless them which persecute you: bless, and curse not.

Rejoice with them that do rejoice, and weep with them that weep.

Be of the same mind one toward another. Mind not high things, but condescend to men of low estate. Be not wise in your own conceits.

Recompense to no man evil for evil. Provide things honest in the sight of all men.

If it be possible, as much as lieth in you, live peaceably with all men. (Romans 12:9-18)

Only one born of the Spirit of God and submitted to His Word can do this. It is beyond the capability of our natural flesh to do so.

God's Word on prayer is aptly summed up in the following:

Confess your faults one to another, and pray one for another, that ye may be healed. The effectual fervent prayer of a righteous man availeth much. (James 5:16)

In other words, for our prayers to have effect, we should confess our sins to one another—especially to one against whom we may have sinned.

This is not the Roman Catholic confessional through which people seek absolution from a "priest," but rather humility before the brethren as a requisite for righteousness.

I should stress that this does not necessarily mean that every sin we commit must be confessed, especially before the entire congregation. However, if we are caught in a particular sin and are hampered in our spiritual growth, or if that sin causes the Body of Christ to suffer, it should be confessed. James 5:16 would also pertain to any sins we feel convicted by the Holy Spirit to confess.

Of course, we must be careful. In today's sin-plagued churches it would be disastrous to confess one's sins openly. To do so would most likely result in self-righteous condemnation and ostracism rather than encouragement grounded in love. We should not confess to just anyone, but to trusted brethren in Christ. And we must exercise discretion, particularly where mixed company is concerned. It would be better if men confessed to trusted men and women to trusted women. If this were done we would be far less likely to sin, knowing that we will be accountable to others. And if all in the assembly were transparent with one another, no one could judge another, knowing that his own sins must also be heard.

Some would argue that our "faults" are not necessarily our sins—they may be our proneness toward making mistakes. But that is not what the Scriptures are talking about. The Greek word translated "faults" in James 5:16 is *paraptomata,* which is properly translated "false step," or "trespass." This is clearly more serious than a fault in one's character or walk with the Lord.

This is a hard saying, difficult to receive for many. I find it difficult myself. But God's Word is clear that confession of our sins will aid our prayers. Yet it seems reasonable that this refers to habitual sin, not an occasional stumbling with which we must all contend.

Recognizing this helps us better understand James 5:14-15:

> *Is any sick among you? let him call for the elders of the assembly; and let them pray over him, anointing him with oil in the name of the Lord:*
>
> *And the prayer of faith shall save the sick, and the Lord shall raise him up; and if he have committed sins, they shall be forgiven him.*

These verses, which immediately precede the command to confess our sins to one another, demonstrate what is expected of the elders—that they be without unconfessed sin themselves. If they are truly elders according to the scriptural requirements, they will be striving to live godly lives and to maintain their ability to pray effectively for those in their care.

Perhaps this is why prayer for the sick is especially entrusted to the elders. They are expected to be living holy lives as a requirement for holding their position. If their prayers are not answered, the elders must examine themselves to see if any sin lies unrepentant in them. Because of the loose standards applied for elder qualification in the churches today, many elders are full of sin themselves, and unable to effectively pray for the sick. Unfortunately, the practice today is to blame the person who is sick, who may or may not be in sin. If the sick person is in sin, we are assured that, with his healing, his sins will be forgiven. But this, too, in the context of the entire passage, implies that the sick person will confess his sins as well.

In any case, it is no more expedient to judge the elders for the lack of healing than it is to judge the one not healed. Sometimes it is by God's design that there is no healing. Each case must be considered on its own merits. Let each judge himself for sin rather than others, unless some sin is openly known. In that case it must be dealt with scripturally.

We see now why Jesus said, "Be ye therefore perfect, even as your Father which is in heaven is perfect" (Matthew 5:48). The word "perfect" (Greek, *teleioi*) signifies having reached maturity.

It is argued that maturity does not equate to sinlessness, but to a general spiritual growth. This is true, as long as we do not lean upon it as an excuse to continue in sin. While we will never be sinless as long as we remain in the flesh, God does expect us to strive for perfection in our spiritual life. Our flesh may continue to wage warfare against our spirit, but we must exercise our own will to resist the flesh:

> *There is therefore now no condemnation to them which are in Christ Jesus, who walk not after the flesh, but after the Spirit.*
>
> *For the law of the Spirit of life in Christ Jesus hath made me free from the law of sin and death.*
>
> *For what the law could not do, in that it was weak through the flesh, God sending his own Son in the likeness of sinful flesh, and for sin, condemned sin in the flesh:*
>
> *That the righteousness of the law might be fulfilled in us, who walk not after the flesh, but after the Spirit.*
>
> *For they that are after the flesh do mind the things of the flesh; but they that are after the Spirit the things of the Spirit.*
>
> *For to be carnally minded is death; but to be spiritually minded is life and peace.*
>
> *Because the carnal mind is enmity against God: for it is not subject to the law of God, neither indeed can be.*
>
> *So then they that are in the flesh cannot please God.*

But ye are not in the flesh, but in the Spirit, if so be that the Spirit of God dwell in you. Now if any man have not the Spirit of Christ, he is none of his.

And if Christ be in you, the body is dead because of sin; but the Spirit is life because of righteousness.

But if the Spirit of him that raised up Jesus from the dead dwell in you, he that raised up Christ from the dead shall also quicken your mortal bodies by his Spirit that dwelleth in you.

Therefore, brethren, we are debtors, not to the flesh, to live after the flesh.

For if ye live after the flesh, ye shall die: but if ye through the Spirit do mortify the deeds of the body, ye shall live.

For as many as are led by the Spirit of God, they are the sons of God. (Romans 8:1-14)

For, brethren, ye have been called unto liberty; only use not liberty for an occasion to the flesh, but by love serve one another.

For all the law is fulfilled in one word, even in this; Thou shalt love thy neighbour as thyself.

But if ye bite and devour one another, take heed that ye be not consumed one of another.

This I say then, Walk in the Spirit, and ye shall not fulfil the lust of the flesh. (Galatians 5:14-16)

Forasmuch then as Christ hath suffered for us in the flesh, arm yourselves likewise with the same mind: for he that hath suffered in the flesh hath ceased from sin;

That he no longer should live the rest of his time in the flesh to the lusts of men, but to the will of God. (1 Peter 4:1-2)

It was not my intention to digress from the subject of prayer to that of holy living. But as we study God's Word on the subject of prayer, we see that it cannot be separated from holy living. Many who adhere to other religions pray they know not to whom. But the same can be said about many who call themselves Christians. They have not grasped the true, holy character of God; they think of Him as some Being who is disposed to meet their demands for comfort in this life rather than as a loving Father who desires them to approach Him with confidence. Holiness (which is really another word for separation from sin and from the love of the world) is God's character; it is also to be the character of His children.

Now, there are times when we are not to pray for others—that is, for relief from their suffering. Why should we pray for a rebellious person? Better that he continue in suffering so that he may recognize his need to surrender to God.

If we are to pray in the Spirit, we must be sensitive to the Spirit's work in others. If God is chastening a brother for his sins, we must agree with that chastening and instruct that brother to repent; otherwise there should be no prayer for his suffering. Yet we do not altogether refrain from praying for him. We should pray that God's work be done in his life.

This is illustrated by Paul's seemingly extreme measure of commanding the Corinthian brethren to turn over to Satan one of their own for the destruction of his flesh so that his spirit might be saved (1 Corinthians 5:5).

In all things, not the least in prayer, we are to be led by the Holy Spirit. Let us therefore examine ourselves to see if we are in the Faith, and if there is anything in our own lives that might be hindering our prayers.

To Whom Do We Pray?

In many prayer settings I have heard brethren praying to "God," "Jesus," and "Holy Spirit." But when the disciples asked Jesus to teach them to pray, what did He say?

> *And he said unto them, When ye pray, say, Our Father which art in heaven...* (Luke 11:2)

Every time Jesus prayed, he called upon His Father. He teaches us in His Word to do the same. What is largely lost to the church world is that Jesus came not just to die for our sins, but to open the way for us to approach the Throne of Grace personally. Prior to His coming the Israelites knew God only as a distant, though loving, Being who spoke to them through their prophets. But it was His intention to send His Son as His emissary to mankind so that all who have faith in His Son would be adopted into His family. He is our Father and the One to whom we look for sustenance. It is an insult to bypass Him and think that we must pray to another—even Jesus. By all means we are not to pray to the Holy Spirit, because His role is to glorify Jesus, not Himself (John 16:13). He speaks to us what He hears from the Father.

Jesus told His disciples that, when He left them they would no longer ask Him for anything, but would ask the Father directly:

> *At that day ye shall ask in my name: and I say not unto you, that I will pray the Father for you:*
> *For the Father himself loveth you, because ye have loved me, and have believed that I came out from God. (John 16:26-27)*

Corporate Prayer

It has been a practice among some—especially in Pentecostal and charismatic churches—for everyone to pray aloud at the same time. I won't judge these people. But if we are to be in agreement with one another, it would be better for each person to pray in turn while the others keep silent. This avoids confusion, and demonstrates courtesy to the one praying. It also allows the whole body to understand the purpose of the prayer.

To Bear One Another's Burdens

> *Brethren, if a man be overtaken in a fault, ye which are spiritual, restore such an one in the spirit of meekness; considering thyself, lest thou also be tempted.*
> *Bear ye one another's burdens, and so fulfil the law of Christ.*
> *For if a man think himself to be something, when he is nothing, he deceiveth himself.*

> *But let every man prove his own work, and then shall he have rejoicing in himself alone, and not in another.*
>
> *For every man shall bear his own burden.* (Galatians 6:1-5)

Intrinsically linked to prayer is the scriptural admonition to bear one another's burdens. This does not mean that we should take another's burden upon ourselves past the point where he can bear the burden himself. Each must be brought to the place where he may begin to bear the burdens of others, and not be a drain upon the resources of those upon whom he must depend for a time.

The Scripture verses above might at first seem contradictory. The problem lies in the words translated "burdens" (v. 2) and "burden" (v. 5). In verse 2, we are commanded to bear one another's burdens (Gr. *baros*: weight, load, burden; something that presses down upon him). In verse 5, we are told that each man must prove his own work or ministry, by bearing his own burden (Gr. *phortion*: a task or service). The task (*phortion*) for each of us, is to bear the burdens (*baros*) of others. It is the law of Christ (love) that is fulfilled when we do this. To not do this is to esteem ourselves too highly, which is contrary to God's Word:

> *Let nothing be done through strife or vainglory; but in lowliness of mind let each esteem other better than themselves.*
>
> *Look not every man on his own things, but every man also on the things of others.* (Philippians 2:3-4)

When Paul speaks of not doing anything through strife, he is saying that we must not be contentious with one another, particularly for the sake of our vanity. Rather, we are to look upon others as better than ourselves. Yet this does not negate the need for contention when it comes to standing for truth or righteousness. If a brother is in sin, or an elder is acting unjustly, each must be confronted with his sin. This will often lead to contention; but if we are on scriptural grounds, and not just contending for contention's sake, or to exert our own will, then the sin of contention falls upon those who refuse scriptural correction.

It is humility before the Lord that causes us to contend for the Faith and for righteousness. This is evidenced by the fact that these verses immediately precede Paul's instructions to have the mind of Christ, which is one of humility.

Let this mind be in you, which was also in Christ Jesus:

Who, being in the form of God, thought it not robbery to be equal with God:

But made himself of no reputation, and took upon him the form of a servant, and was made in the likeness of men:

And being found in fashion as a man, he humbled himself, and became obedient unto death, even the death of the cross. (Philippians 2:5-8)

So we see that our heavenly Father wants us to be obedient, just as Jesus was obedient. For this is the evidence of our humility. Yet outward piety is in itself insufficient for conformity to the law of love. All things must be done by faith, relying upon the Holy Spirit to convict us of the need to conform to God's Word where we might be lacking, and then respond accordingly.

There are many areas in which we must bear one another's burdens, and often this requires a great deal of sacrifice on our part. With the present-day emphasis upon psychological theory that sets boundaries for service lest we be taken advantage of, it is easy to find excuses not to help others. But Scripture doesn't set boundaries.

What doth it profit, my brethren, though a man say he hath faith, and have not works? can faith save him?

If a brother or sister be naked, and destitute of daily food,

And one of you say unto them, Depart in peace, be ye warmed and filled; notwithstanding ye give them

*not those things which are needful to the body; what
doth it profit?*

*Even so faith, if it hath not works, is dead, being
alone.* (James 2:14-17)

How often do believers have the means to help a brother or
sister who, through no fault of their own, is in need, yet they
guard it greedily. They allow themselves to be put under the
burden of tithing to their church, but give little or nothing
beyond that because they consider it the church's responsibility
to provide for the brethren. This is no different than relying
upon the welfare state to take care of those whose care is
legitimately charged to the family.

In some cases it is advisable to take advantage of the
welfare offered through the state. But as much as is in our power
as believers in Christ, we should not be party to perpetuating a
system that has usurped the role of the family and of the
assembly in meeting the needs of our relations.

Give to the assembly (if it has a legitimate need) or to other
ministries as the Lord leads, but do not neglect that He may be
leading you to give to your brother also. And do not consider the
tithe as binding upon you, but rather follow the Lord's
instruction not to let your left hand know what your right hand
is doing (do not keep track—Matthew 6:3). Follow also Paul's
instruction to give cheerfully, not grudgingly, as you have
determined within your heart (2 Corinthians 9:7).

If you lend to a brother in Christ do not demand
repayment. If a brother lends or gives to you, do your best to pay
it back. Expect nothing from others, but act so that they may
expect everything from you. In this way we will fulfill the law of
love, not counting our relationships by their dollar value.

To Minister To Those In Need

*And let us not be weary in well doing: for in due
season we shall reap, if we faint not.*

*As we have therefore opportunity, let us do good
unto all men, especially unto them who are of the
household of faith.* (Galatians 6:9-10)

An important function of the assembly is to care for its members. In contrast to bearing one another's burdens, this is corporate ministry, not individual.

Yet because the modern churches are largely impersonal, the needs of individuals often go unnoticed. People are reticent to seek help from strangers. And a congregation whose leadership stands somewhat aloof will inspire few genuinely hurting people to seek help, whether spiritual or temporal. Often the closest contact people have to their pastor is limited to a handshake at the door. And that is meant for them to compliment him on his eloquence rather than to seek solace for their particular need. Of course, they are allowed to make an appointment for counseling.

Benevolence committees help where they can, but those in charge are also often strangers to the vast majority of congregants—especially in large churches. Fellowships that multiply themselves into more fellowships at the point when they begin to become less personal are more able to minister to the needs of one another. They are also more intimidating to people who do not want to get too intimately known. But this latter problem is not really a problem for true believers who see the need to sacrifice themselves for others.

When one's needs are made known to the fellowship, it should be determined by the elders how best to meet those needs, whether spiritual, financial or of any other nature. In all cases, wisdom is paramount. We may do more harm than good by seeking to alleviate every adverse condition unconditionally.

Is a brother attempting to help himself without being a burden to others? Or is he taking advantage of the brethren?

> *For even when we were with you, this we commanded you, that if any would not work, neither should he eat.*
>
> *For we hear that there are some which walk among you disorderly, working not at all, but are busybodies.*
>
> *Now them that are such we command and exhort by our Lord Jesus Christ, that with quietness they work, and eat their own bread.*

But ye, brethren, be not weary in well doing.

And if any man obey not our word by this epistle, note that man, and have no company with him, that he may be ashamed.

Yet count him not as an enemy, but admonish him as a brother. (2 Thessalonians 3:10-15)

Are families helping one another? Are elderly parents being cared for by their children? Are fathers providing for their families' needs? Family members must be held accountable if they are not providing for their own:

But if any provide not for his own, and specially for those of his own house, he hath denied the faith, and is worse than an infidel. (1 Timothy 5:8)

Are widows seeking aid truly widows, lacking support from family members and meeting scriptural guidelines?

Honour widows that are widows indeed.

But if any widow have children or nephews, let them learn first to shew piety at home, and to requite their parents: for that is good and acceptable before God.

Now she that is a widow indeed, and desolate, trusteth in God, and continueth in supplications and prayers night and day.

But she that liveth in pleasure is dead while she liveth. (1 Timothy 5:3-6)

Let not a widow be taken into the number under threescore years old, having been the wife of one man,

Well reported of for good works; if she have brought up children, if she have lodged strangers, if she have washed the saints' feet, if she have relieved the afflicted, if she have diligently followed every good work.

But the younger widows refuse: for when they have begun to wax wanton against Christ, they will marry;

Having damnation, because they have cast off their first faith.

And withal they learn to be idle, wandering about from house to house; and not only idle, but tattlers also and busybodies, speaking things which they ought not.

I will therefore that the younger women marry, bear children, guide the house, give none occasion to the adversary to speak reproachfully.

For some are already turned aside after Satan.

If any man or woman that believeth have widows, let them relieve them, and let not the assembly be charged; that it may relieve them that are widows indeed. (1 Timothy 3:9-16)

These seem like harsh words for widows that remarry. But this condemnation was not for all widows; it was for those who had taken vows of service to God and were receiving aid from the assembly. They broke those vows, thus breaking faith with God and with the assembly.

All of these questions factor into the decision of whether to help and how much to help. In any case, it is up to godly elders, guided by Scripture and the Holy Spirit, to make the final decisions in these matters.

Generosity coupled with prudence should mark the charity of an assembly just as it should that of individuals. Limited help to those outside the Body of Christ may also be allowed, provided the same criteria apply.

5
Leadership

As we look at leadership in the assembly we will deal with areas that are highly controversial. I wish to state at the outset that what is written here is the product of several years of Scripture study and experience in the Body of Christ.

It is submitted with the caveat that everything be tested by God's Word and not by the particular theological understanding that one has attained. Whether one identifies as a Calvinist, an Arminian, a fundamentalist, a charismatic, a Pentecostal, or whatever one calls oneself, I urge all to set aside their cherished theological biases and examine everything by their own study of God's Word.

This writing has already been submitted to several biblically literate brethren of various persuasions. Although not all agreed with everything, all are to a large degree in agreement with this writing as a whole. I thank them for their insights and encouragement. I pray that this attempt to bring light on the subject of leadership may be of some value to the Body of Christ.

And he gave some, apostles; and some, prophets; and some, evangelists; and some, pastors and teachers;

For the perfecting of the saints, for the work of the ministry, for the edifying of the body of Christ:

> *Till we all come in the unity of the faith, and of the knowledge of the Son of God, unto a perfect man, unto the measure of the stature of the fullness of Christ:*
>
> *That we henceforth be no more children, tossed to and fro, and carried about with every wind of doctrine, by the sleight of men, and cunning craftiness, whereby they lie in wait to deceive;*
>
> *But speaking the truth in love, may grow up into him in all things, which is the head, even Christ:*
>
> *From whom the whole body fitly joined together and compacted by that which every joint supplieth, according to the effectual working in the measure of every part, maketh increase of the body unto the edifying of itself in love.* (Ephesians 4:11-16)

The adage, "No man is an island unto himself" is best exemplified within the assembly of the saints of God. Not only can man not come to full maturity in his social, business and other human endeavors without proper leadership, the believer in Christ cannot come to maturity in the Faith without submission to proper leadership within the Body of Christ.

Note the word "proper." Many have encountered experiences in their churches that have been at or near two extremes:

- Authoritarian, sometimes even cult-like, domination by spiritual leaders;

- Insufficient discipleship and improper application of God's Word to fully equip the saints in their quest for attainment of Christlikeness.

Both experiences often result in loss of faith in Christ and an aversion to authority. At best they may result in immaturity and lack of understanding of what God requires of His people. Both work contrary to the interests of the individual and of the Body of Christ as a whole. For those who do not completely cast off faith in Christ, these extremes can lead toward a go-it-alone attitude.

There are many who claim that they don't need to be in fellowship, at least not on a regular basis. Everything they've encountered in the churches has discouraged them from trusting in leadership within the Body of Christ.

What they really mean is that they don't need improper leadership. And they are correct. But they are wrong if they think they can continue to walk apart from the Body of Christ and still attain to spiritual maturity.

> *And let us consider one another to provoke unto love and to good works:*
>
> *Not forsaking the assembling of ourselves together, as the manner of some is; but exhorting one another: and so much the more, as ye see the day approaching.* (Hebrews 10:24-25)

Apart from isolation imposed against one's will, it isn't enough to study God's Word on one's own and keep to oneself, for that would be contrary to the Scriptures one claims to believe. While the Holy Spirit may give insight through personal study, it is not God's will that His children grow up unattended and without opportunities to be ministered to, and to minister to others.

The purpose of leadership is to provide the means by which God's people may be fitly joined together, bringing about the unity of the Faith that will strengthen the corporate body as well as the individual.

> *Iron sharpeneth iron; so a man sharpeneth the countenance of his friend.* (Proverbs 27:17)

> *Now there are diversities of gifts, but the same Spirit.*
>
> *And there are differences of administrations, but the same Lord.*
>
> *And there are diversities of operations, but it is the same God which worketh all in all.*
>
> *But the manifestation of the Spirit is given to every man to profit withal.*

For to one is given by the Spirit the word of wisdom; to another the word of knowledge by the same Spirit;

To another faith by the same Spirit; to another the gifts of healing by the same Spirit;

To another the working of miracles; to another prophecy; to another discerning of spirits; to another divers kinds of tongues; to another the interpretation of tongues:

But all these worketh that one and the selfsame Spirit, dividing to every man severally as he will.

For as the body is one, and hath many members, and all the members of that one body, being many, are one body: so also is Christ.

For by one Spirit are we all baptized into one body, whether we be Jews or Gentiles, whether we be bond or free; and have been all made to drink into one Spirit.

For the body is not one member, but many.

If the foot shall say, Because I am not the hand, I am not of the body; is it therefore not of the body?

And if the ear shall say, Because I am not the eye, I am not of the body; is it therefore not of the body?

If the whole body were an eye, where were the hearing? If the whole were hearing, where were the smelling?

But now hath God set the members every one of them in the body, as it hath pleased him.

And if they were all one member, where were the body?

But now are they many members, yet but one body.

And the eye cannot say unto the hand, I have no need of thee: nor again the head to the feet, I have no need of you.

Nay, much more those members of the body, which seem to be more feeble, are necessary:

And those members of the body, which we think to be less honourable, upon these we bestow more abundant honour; and our uncomely parts have more abundant comeliness.

For our comely parts have no need: but God hath tempered the body together, having given more abundant honour to that part which lacked:

That there should be no schism in the body; but that the members should have the same care one for another.

And whether one member suffer, all the members suffer with it; or one member be honoured, all the members rejoice with it.

Now ye are the body of Christ, and members in particular. (1 Corinthians 12:4-27)

Every member of Christ's Body is important to the whole. Every member has been gifted by God to contribute to what is lacking in all the other members.

It is up to the leadership to cultivate the gifts of the individual members. Leadership has largely failed to do this, preferring instead to cultivate the natural talents of worldly-wise people. They have mistaken natural talent for spiritual gifts, often because they have relied upon currently popular psychologically-based "spiritual gifts" surveys.

Because of this failure on the part of leadership, true believers are discouraged from continuing under that leadership's direction.

Paul's lesson in 1 Corinthians 12 does not end at delineating the importance of every member of the Body. For he places that importance within the context of submission to proper leadership:

And God hath set some in the church, first apostles, secondarily prophets, thirdly teachers, after that miracles, then gifts of healings, helps, governments, diversities of tongues.

Are all apostles? are all prophets? are all teachers? are all workers of miracles?

Have all the gifts of healing? do all speak with tongues? do all interpret?

But covet earnestly the best gifts: and yet shew I unto you a more excellent way. (1 Corinthians 12:28-31)

The more excellent way is love as outlined in Chapter 13. Yet even love cannot be fully manifested in an individual believer's life unless that believer is functioning within the Body of Christ.

Certainly he may be able to do good works motivated by love; he may be able to accomplish much in the way of personal growth and understanding of God's Word. But apart from the Body of Christ he will never attain to the full stature of maturity that God intends. He will always be lacking.

Unfortunately, many are finding themselves separated from congregational life, not because they want to be, but because they have lost confidence in the leadership. They have come to realize that just because men **ordain** other men as leaders, it doesn't mean that God has **anointed** those men as leaders. There is a great difference between ordination and anointing.

POSITIONS

The proper term for this heading should probably be "Ministries," rather than "Positions." In considering this, I felt that, for lack of a better term, that of "positions" delineates between the anointed position for a particular ministry as an elder as opposed to a particular gift that may be performed by any member of the Body of Christ. For example, the position of evangelist is conferred upon one who meets the qualifications of an elder, and whose gifting is for the proclaiming of the Gospel as a whole. This is contrasted with the gifting of ministering the Gospel given on occasion to other members of the Body. So the term positions must be understood within this context.

As in so many other areas, leadership in the churches has been founded on erroneous presuppositions and traditions that are, at best, unsupported by God's Word and, at worst, contrary to God's Word. Whereas English Bibles use the term "office" for these positions, it is, again, the result of hierarchical influence. There is no Greek word for "office" in Scripture. The term was inserted in order to bolster the authority of the church hierarchies. In Romans 11:13 the word for deacon (*diakonian* "service") is translated "office," and in Romans 12:4 the word for function (*praxin*) is translated "office." These are the only stand-alone uses of any Greek word that is translated "office." All other uses of "office' are inserted.

It is often assumed that the only remaining positions from among those enumerated in Ephesians 4:11 and 1 Corinthians 12 are those of the pastor-teacher and the evangelist. This assumption is based largely on a misunderstanding of these positions as they relate to the local body.

Whether Paul was speaking in Ephesians 4:11 of one position called "pastor-teacher," or two distinct positions—one called "pastor," the other "teacher"—is debated. Many of today's pastors prefer to claim the combined title. This makes little difference, simply because all elders must be able to teach. In fact, the position of pastor is not even mentioned in 1 Corinthians 12, whereas all the other positions are.

In most churches today, all of the positions are embodied in one person, called the pastor, who assumes the duties of apostle, prophet, evangelist, pastor, teacher, worship leader, head of elders and deacons, CEO, and all-around Jack-of-all-trades in spiritual and temporal matters.

In effect, today's pastors are not far removed from the role of priests. In the Roman Catholic tradition there is a priesthood that stands between the people and God. At the head of that priesthood is the pope who presides over the College of Cardinals. These comprise the oversight for the Holy See and the pastorate of the Universal Church headquartered in Rome. Under the pope and cardinals are the archbishops, followed by the bishops, then by the senior pastors of parishes, and lastly by the parish priests. In some parishes, particularly in non-Catholic countries, some laypersons (men and women) considered worthy may be appointed as deacons and deaconesses.

The hierarchical structure of the Roman Church set the tone for the Protestant churches simply because the majority of the Protestant Reformers were Roman Catholic priests or intellectuals who "protested" certain unscriptural doctrines and practices of Romanism.

In spite of their faults we owe much to the Reformers for their courage in standing up to the corrupt and apostate religious system of Rome. Their stories are legend. However, the Reformation may be seen as merely the first major step in God's removing those of His people who were caught in the apostasy of Roman Catholicism. There were, of course, believers who were never caught in that apostasy. Later attempts to refine the "protest" along more scriptural lines relative to other doctrines were also steps in that removal process. Each breaking away from prior imperfections has contributed to a more pure understanding of God's Word and purpose for His people.

Yet as blessed as the churches have been as a result of the Reformation and its subsequent refinements, the seeds of their own destruction were sown by the ignorance and religious traditions of the Reformers. Beginning with pure motives, the movements have fallen into apostasy, some to a greater degree than others.

The reason for this is the hierarchical clergy-oriented structure of the Protestant churches and those denominations (and independent churches) that came out of them. Such a structure, being contrary to God's plan for His *ekklesia*, often generates lack of confidence in the average believer for being able to boldly approach the Throne of Grace (Hebrews 4:16) and to take full advantage of his freedom in Christ. He doesn't think he can function without the pastor's direction and counsel.

The religious establishment has propagated an unholy clergy-oriented leadership that has effectively kept the plurality of eldership at bay. Professional clergy have replaced the anointed positions of apostles, prophets, evangelists, shepherds and teachers with the single position of pastor. All others function in name only—if at all; the true elders for the most part are sitting in the pews with nothing to do.

For centuries young men fresh out of seminaries have been put in positions of authority over, and as teachers to, aged men whose years of walking with the Lord far exceed the years the new pastor has lived life on this earth.

By God's grace many pastors have managed to become capable leaders and godly shepherds. But they have done so because their hearts were right, even if their training was faulty. We cannot always blame pastors for the predicament they are in simply because they were trained to assume their role.

I say God bless those pastors who have survived the stress and difficulties of having come from seminary still wet behind the ears, only to be placed by their denominations as elders to godly men in their seventies and eighties.

The pastors are no more to blame than is the system that foisted that life-long difficulty upon them.

Some have borne up well under the strain and have remained faithful to their flocks, sacrificing many hours and even their health for the sake of often unruly congregants who don't understand the first thing about godliness no matter how much they've been taught.

Others (far too many) have cracked under the strain. They've lost their families, their positions and their reputations. The difficulties they've endured do not excuse them for their sins, but those standing on the outside should be ready to offer compassion and understanding when a pastor falls, provided he demonstrates repentance.

However, this was never intended by the Lord when He founded His *ekklesia*. The present situation has given rise to many abuses not only against the people, but against the pastors themselves.

The perils that accompany the present-day form of leadership within the churches have been amply demonstrated over the centuries. There are too many stories of pastors who started out with pure motives only to fall into sexual sin with women (often married women) in their congregations because the pastors took on the role of counselor to those women.

Scripture places the responsibility for oversight of the women on their husbands, fathers, brothers and other male relatives. In the Body of Christ the elder women are to teach the younger women what God expects of them as wives and mothers (Titus 2:3-5).

Another problem has been the naïveté of pastors, raised in their church's theological system, unable to discern error.

The pressure under the current system also results in burnout for many pastors who are unable to keep pace with such a grueling task, especially in large churches. Burnout from one man assuming all the tasks that Scripture assigns to different elders is common.

Pride and carelessness ensue for men who are looked up to as exclusive—or near exclusive—disseminators of God's Word in a congregation. This is why the Lord wisely chose to establish a plurality of diverse leadership known as elders.

ELDERS

Due to tradition, there has been a distinction made between the idea of elder as opposed to that of bishop. Just as the church-appointed translators of the English Bibles mistranslated the word *ekklesia* in keeping with the hierarchical mandate, so the word *episkopon* has been mistranslated as "bishop." The position of bishop, replete with pomp and circumstance, clerical collars, flowing robes and mitered hats, is not scriptural. This is another invention of Roman Catholicism taken from paganism.

In some Protestant congregations, particularly within the "high church" denominations such as the Lutheran, Episcopalian, Eastern Orthodox, etc., there are bishops assigned to oversee the parish pastors. The heady nature of "bishopry" has now even infected some of the charismatic churches.

The Greek *episkopon* is more properly translated "overseer." Scripture demonstrates that *episkopon*, mistranslated "bishop," is synonymous with that of *presbuterou*—"elder:"

> For this cause left I thee in Crete, that thou shouldest set in order the things that are wanting, and ordain elders [presbuteros] in every city, as I had appointed thee:
> If any be blameless, the husband of one wife, having faithful children not accused of riot or unruly.

For a bishop [episkopon—"overseer"] *must be blameless, as the steward of God; not selfwilled, not soon angry, not given to wine, no striker, not given to filthy lucre;*

But a lover of hospitality, a lover of good men, sober, just, holy, temperate;

Holding fast the faithful word as he hath been taught, that he may be able by sound doctrine both to exhort and to convince the gainsayers. (Titus 1:5-9)

So the function of a "bishop" should properly be that of merely an "overseer"—one among several elders—not some hiarchical officer. The role of overseer is properly assigned to all the elders who care for the assemblies and minister to the people's spiritual needs.

In view of the consistent use of "overseer" to describe the duties of elders by Paul in his letters to both Timothy and Titus (especially where he equates the two in the same passage), this should put to final rest any notion of "bishops" as commonly understood.

The apostles, prophets, evangelists, shepherds and teachers are all elders. Because of the centuries-old misuse of the term and position of bishop as one of higher rank, it is more advantageous to use the term "overseer" or "elder" today. Primarily, we'll use "elder."

The term "elder" comes from the Greek *presbuterou*, meaning someone who is older in terms of age. It has a secondary meaning which connotes higher rank. In Israel the elders were the learned men of the Sanhedrin, as well as the administrators of the city. All were expected to be of impeccable character and reliable in the administration of their duties. They rightly deserved special honor among the people. The fact that the elders of Israel did not attain that position easily or at a young age contributed to the synonymous usage of the term elder for both age and wisdom in the Faith.

It is not to be any less the case in the assembly. Yet in spite of Scripture's wisdom in delineating the leadership of the assembly as a plurality of elders with no one in preeminence, in today's churches the leadership is generally made up of certain positions whose authority is in descending rank according to the following order:

- Pastor

- Associate or assistant pastor(s)

- Elders

- Deacons

Within this context the pastors are considered elders and are generally professional clergy (i.e., paid staff). There is usually a senior pastor and associate and/or assistant pastors who may or may not be on the paid pastoral staff.

In the churches the elders are usually elected by the congregation or appointed by the pastor. Usually, they hold their position for a specific term (one or two years, or at the behest of the pastor), then must be reelected or reappointed.

The deacons are seldom considered elders, but usually hold their positions in much the same manner, being elected or appointed for specific terms. Some may be hired by the senior pastor as full-time janitors and/or handymen.

From where did the practice of rotating the elders come? Certainly Scripture does not suggest that the position of an elder is subject to reelection. When does a man cease to be an elder? An elder is an elder for life unless he sins and fails to repent. Even if an elder sins it should be the object of the fellowship to restore him, not to discard him. After he can no longer function in his position due to age or disability he should still be honored as an elder.

Neither the position of "elder" nor that of "deacon," as they are acquired and maintained in most of the churches today, are scriptural. They are born out of Protestant tradition which is only slightly removed from that of Roman Catholicism.

Scripture does make a distinction between elders and deacons when we consider together 1 Timothy 3:1-8 and Titus 5:7. The qualifications for both elders and deacons are virtually identical, except that elders must be able to teach.

It is often assumed that Acts 6:2 differentiates between elders and deacons, the elders being charged with the spiritual welfare of the congregation and the deacons being charged with its temporal welfare. However, this passage merely relates that the twelve apostles decided that it was not suitable for *them* to be burdened with mundane tasks, but that they should be able to give themselves over to fasting and prayer, and let others who were spiritually qualified take on those tasks:

> *Then the twelve called the multitude of the disciples unto them, and said, It is not reason that we should leave the word of God, and serve tables.*
>
> *Wherefore, brethren, look ye out among you seven men of honest report, full of the Holy Ghost and wisdom, whom we may appoint over this business.*
>
> *But we will give ourselves continually to prayer, and to the ministry of the word.*
>
> *And the saying pleased the whole multitude: and they chose Stephen, a man full of faith and of the Holy Ghost, and Philip, and Prochorus, and Nicanor, and Timon, and Parmenas, and Nicolas a proselyte of Antioch:*
>
> *Whom they set before the apostles: and when they had prayed, they laid their hands on them.* (Acts 6:2-6)

It appears as if at least some of these seven men may have been elders charged with the responsibility to administer the temporal needs of the assembly in Jerusalem. Certainly, as we see the mighty deeds of Stephen in the following verses, it must be concluded that he was an elder and not merely some table server.

The idea of serving tables is obviously a figure of speech, as it was highly unlikely that the apostles were actually waiting on tables. They were no doubt referring to the duty of administering the funds for support of widows and other mundane tasks.

There is certainly nothing to suggest that, in this instance, at least some chosen were not elders. If they were elders, this throws a new light on their duties as opposed to those of the twelve. Yet Scripture does make a distinction between elders and deacons in the assembly based upon their qualifications.

Qualifications For Elders

> *This is a true saying, If a man desire the [position] of an elder, he desireth a good work.*
>
> *An elder then must be blameless, the husband of one wife, vigilant, sober, of good behaviour, given to hospitality, apt to teach;*
>
> *Not given to wine, no striker, not greedy of filthy lucre; but patient, not a brawler, not covetous;*
>
> *One that ruleth well his own house, having his children in subjection with all gravity;*
>
> *(For if a man know not how to rule his own house, how shall he take care of the assembly of God?)*
>
> *Not a novice, lest being lifted up with pride he fall into the condemnation of the devil.*
>
> *Moreover he must have a good report of them which are without; lest he fall into reproach and the snare of the devil.* (1 Timothy 3:1-7)

These qualifications are necessary for all elders. Given these strict requirements according to God's Word, it is little wonder that many true believers in the churches are concerned about the condition of their leaders. Few men in the first-century assemblies met these qualifications. How fewer meet them today after having been so far removed from the authority of the original apostles?

Many pastors cannot control their own children, yet they will not relinquish their livelihood for the sake of scriptural purity. Many elders are appointed or elected according to their natural talents, popularity, or even financial standing, rather than according to biblical qualifications. Perhaps in some churches no one would meet these qualifications. Then why are they functioning as churches except that they have a franchise charter from a denominational corporation and/or a government license?

As for filthy lucre, mammon plays a central role in many churches.

How many pastors are not self-willed, or do not quickly become angry when challenged for their unscriptural teachings?

Sober? Just? Holy? Temperate? How lacking in these qualities are so many men leading the churches today.

As for holding fast the faithful Word, or being able by sound doctrine to exhort and convince the gainsayers, many of today's pastors are least qualified in these areas, and many purposely avoid these things, even refusing to exhort or expose those whose teachings are subverting the faith of many believers. This is another reason why so many brethren are leaving the churches. Their leaders have no zeal for truth. They are afraid of men rather than afraid of God.

Yet as bleak as things look, God has not abandoned His people. The true elders are among us; it is up to the assembly to recognize them and give them the honor they deserve, submitting to them in all spiritual matters. But this will mean coming out from among the apostate churches and forming new fellowships based upon the clear instruction of God's Word as opposed to the traditions of men.

This will take courage and will certainly incur the wrath of the religious establishment. But so be it if Christ is our Head.

Duties Of Elders

> *The elders which are among you I exhort, who am also an elder, and a witness of the sufferings of Christ, and also a partaker of the glory that shall be revealed:*
>
> *Feed the flock of God which is among you, taking the oversight thereof, not by constraint, but willingly; not for filthy lucre, but of a ready mind;*
>
> *Neither as being lords over God's heritage, but being ensamples to the flock.* (1 Peter 5:1-3)

The elders are commissioned to oversee the assembly, which means they are to keep the flock in line with God's Word. They are not to keep it in line with their particular agenda or religious tradition. This is why Peter says they are not to lord it over the flock; they are to be true servants in their hearts and in their actions. How different this is to the role taken by many pastors today.

When Peter says they should feed the flock he implies that they are all shepherds to some degree, although the position of shepherd will be seen to be unique to the other positions.

Obviously, pure motives are essential to the duties of elders. Constraint does not mean merely functioning under protest; it also means functioning without pure motives. The need to maintain a livelihood motivates many pastors who should otherwise leave their positions. This is particularly true of pastors who have had little or no experience in earning a living outside of their religious vocation.

The professional pastor is often placed in the position of functioning under such constraint. This is why it would be better if leadership were held by men who were also laborers in the secular work force, whether as self-employed or as employees of others.

They would not be a burden and drain upon the resources of the assembly. And they would be better able to identify with the people's struggles to maintain their households. Perhaps this would keep them from placing financial burdens upon the flock to fund their particular "visions."

Church hierarchies are not far removed from government bureaucracies in their attitudes toward "the little people." They just don't identify well with the masses who support them.

If things were done scripturally, and no one man were preeminent, each would share in the labors within the fellowship.

For this they might receive additional income according to the desires of the assembly as reflected in their giving for that specific purpose. But nowhere in Scripture is a professional clergy required or even hinted at. On the contrary, to work with one's hands proves one's worthiness to lead:

> For ye know what commandments we gave you by the Lord Jesus.
> For this is the will of God, even your sanctification, that ye should abstain from fornication:

> *That every one of you should know how to possess his vessel in sanctification and honour;...*
> *And that ye study to be quiet, and to do your own business, and to work with your own hands, as we commanded you;*
> *That ye may walk honestly toward them that are without, and that ye may have lack of nothing.* (1 Thessalonians 4:2-12)

Some professional pastors will argue that this applies to the rest of the congregation, not to them. Unless there is some scriptural proof for their position apart from the church tradition of maintaining a professional clergy, they have no basis for this claim. In fact, Scripture, in its consistency, would indicate the opposite. A requirement for an elder is that he have a good report among unbelievers:

> *Moreover he must have a good report of them which are without; lest he fall into reproach and the snare of the devil.* (1 Timothy 3:7)

In 1 Thessalonians 4:11-12, cited above, the way in which a believer maintains a good report among unbelievers is by working with his own hands.

The world values honest labor. And while oversight of the people of God may be considered honest labor by some believers, it is not always so with unbelievers. In view of the many scandals involving money by church leaders and televangelists, it is all the more important today that God's people—leadership included— work honestly to support themselves apart from their service to the Body of Christ.

But wouldn't this mean that they wouldn't have time to handle the administration of their church? With all the duties pastors perform today don't they need to be fully supported?

Again, most pastors are functioning unscripturally today; all of their duties should be shared by others who are qualified to do so. This would mean sacrificing their prestige, but it would avoid power trips. It would also mean that the flock would not be in the hands of one fallible man.

Better that several fallible men keep checks and balances upon each other than that one fallible man have all the power. Isn't that one of the issues protested by the Reformers about the pope? Yet so many men today want to be little popes over whatever portion of God's people they can attain authority.

> *Where no counsel is, the people fall: but in the multitude of counsellors there is safety.* (Proverbs 11:14)

Those who argue for a professional clergy cite 1 Timothy 5:17-18:

> *Let the elders that rule well be counted worthy of double honour, especially they who labour in the word and doctrine.*
> *For the scripture saith, Thou shalt not muzzle the ox that treadeth out the corn. And, The labourer is worthy of his reward.*

The idea of rendering honor to those in leadership is scriptural, but honor does not necessarily mean money.

The Greek word for "honour" is *time* (tee-may), which may mean either dignity or something of material value. It is the same word used in Romans 9:21:

> *Hath not the potter power over the clay, of the same lump to make one vessel unto honour, and another unto dishonour?*

It is also used in 1 Timothy 6:1 for slaves honoring their masters:

> *Let as many servants as are under the yoke count their own masters worthy of all honour, that the name of God and his doctrine be not blasphemed.*

In most instances where this word is used it refers to esteem and dignity being given, not money.

However, a workman is worthy of his labor (1 Timothy 5:18). And Paul even told the Corinthian believers that he labored among them without pay as a matter of his own choice, not as a matter of lack of responsibility on their part.

By all means, the people should compensate the leadership for their service to the Body of Christ. Yet they should not have to do so out of compulsion or tradition, but out of willing hearts. Not to do so would demonstrate a selfish attitude, willing to take, but not to give. For those who cannot give money, they should give service, perhaps working on the elders' homes or some such thing. But all should give cheerfully and without compulsion, for the Lord loves a cheerful giver (2 Corinthians 9:7).

So Scripture does indicate that it is proper to render monetary support for the elders. But this would logically mean all the elders, not just the pastor. Nor does it necessarily mean total support as a livelihood.

Now, sometimes total support, at least for a time, may be necessary, depending upon the extensiveness of one's ministry to the fellowship. This is a matter of conscience for not only the elders, but for the assembly as a whole. Monetary reward should not be a consideration for one who desires to minister. Rather, those who receive the benefit of the ministry should be willing to reward those who serve them.

Those ministers who absolutely refuse to receive compensation should be commended. But sometimes that refusal may be based upon pride. Whatever the case, all parties should examine themselves to ascertain the motives of their own hearts in both giving and receiving ministry and compensation.

In the underground assembly it may be impossible to maintain a paid ministry, or it may be necessary to support the elders. Survival may dictate any number of scenarios. Let us be open to the Holy Spirit's direction in these matters. Yet overall, it would be best for the elders to serve without compensation.

Selection of Elders

How one becomes an elder is a matter of debate in the churches. As stated earlier, the idea of a "bishop" in today's churches is far removed from the scriptural model of an elder.

So-called elders in today's churches are usually appointed by senior pastors or elected by the congregation.

Scripture indicates that the appointment of elders is up to the apostles:

> *And there came thither certain Jews from Antioch and Iconium, who persuaded the people, and, having stoned Paul, drew him out of the city, supposing he had been dead.*
>
> *Howbeit, as the disciples stood round about him, he rose up, and came into the city: and the next day he departed with Barnabas to Derbe.*
>
> *And when they had preached the gospel to that city, and had taught many, they returned again to Lystra, and to Iconium, and Antioch,*
>
> *Confirming the souls of the disciples, and exhorting them to continue in the faith, and that we must through much tribulation enter into the kingdom of God.*
>
> *And when they had ordained them elders in every assembly, and had prayed with fasting, they commended them to the Lord, on whom they believed.*
> (Acts 14:19-23)

Here we see that Paul and Barnabas appointed the elders for all the assemblies in Derbe. Paul claimed the position of apostle. Also, Acts 14:14 calls Barnabas an apostle; it is certainly obvious that he performed the duties of an apostle in the oversight of the new assemblies.

The same is true of Timothy whom Paul exhorted to rule well over the assemblies in his care. Although Scripture does not outright name Timothy as an apostle, it was up to him to appoint and oversee the elders. This is strongly implied by Paul's instruction to Timothy to not lightly receive an accusation against an elder:

> *Against an elder receive not an accusation, but before two or three witnesses.*

Them that sin rebuke before all, that others also may fear.

I charge thee before God, and the Lord Jesus Christ, and the elect angels, that thou observe these things without preferring one before another, doing nothing by partiality.

Lay hands suddenly on no man, neither be partaker of other men's sins: keep thyself pure. (1 Timothy 5:19-22)

These words indicate that Timothy acted as an apostle in laying hands on those appointed as elders, and in overseeing them. Were he not in a position of authority as an apostle over the other elders he would not have been cautioned against easily accepting accusations against them, or been encouraged to rebuke those who sinned.

It becomes clear, then, that while the apostles are also subject to the scrutiny of the elders as a whole, there is a specific anointing that accompanies the position of an apostle. The apostle is, in a sense, the elder to the elders. Yet, again, all are to be subject to one another.

As we look at the various elders we will see the distinctions of their specific positions.

APOSTLES

The term apostle derives from the Greek, *apostolos*, lit., "one sent forth" (*apo*, "from," + *stello*, "to send"). The word is used of the Lord to describe His relation to God, (Hebrews. 3:1). The original twelve chosen by the Lord were called apostles. Paul, though he had encountered the Lord Jesus on the road to Damascus, had not "companied with" the Lord "all the time" of His earthly ministry, and hence was not eligible for a place among them, according to Peter's description of the necessary qualifications (Acts 1:22). Paul was commissioned directly by the Lord Himself to carry the Gospel to the Gentiles.

It is argued that there are no apostles today; the position was done away after the original apostles died.

It is true that there are no apostles of the same stature of Paul and the other twelve who had personal encounters with Jesus. But nowhere in Scripture are we told that apostles are only those who walked with the Lord. This is a presupposition based upon cessation theology.

We must, of course, make a distinction between the original apostles and those who followed after. The prerequisites for the apostolic council of the original assembly at Jerusalem were set forth by Peter in calling for one to replace Judas:

> *For it is written in the book of Psalms, Let his habitation be desolate, and let no man dwell therein: and his bishoprick [oversight] let another take.*
>
> *Wherefore of these men which have companied with us all the time that the Lord Jesus went in and out among us,*
>
> *Beginning from the baptism of John, unto that same day that he was taken up from us, must one be ordained to be a witness with us of his resurrection.*
>
> *And they appointed two, Joseph called Barsabas, who was surnamed Justus, and Matthias.*
>
> *And they prayed, and said, Thou, Lord, which knowest the hearts of all men, shew whether of these two thou hast chosen,*
>
> *That he may take part of this ministry and apostleship, from which Judas by transgression fell, that he might go to his own place.*
>
> *And they gave forth their lots; and the lot fell upon Matthias; and he was numbered with the eleven apostles.* (Acts 1:20-26)

The apostles saw the need to replace Judas with another who had been a witness of the Lord's Resurrection, the focal point of true faith in Jesus. Only those who were witnesses of the Resurrection could serve as authorities over the whole Body of Christ. They alone could define the Faith and set the standards for the assemblies not only in that age, but in the ages to follow. With their writings of the post-messianic Scriptures, the Body of Christ was given that witness for all time. Now it is up to those following in the footsteps of the apostles to carry on those truths through faithfulness to their written testimonies. Those who seek to change, add to, or subtract from, their writings are false teachers.

Those who argue for the original eleven plus Paul as the only apostles do not recognize Matthias as an apostle, but as an unauthorized appointee by the original apostles after Judas' death. They believe that the Lord chose Paul to replace Judas. However, Scripture, written by inspiration of the Holy Spirit, indicates no fault with the assembly's choice, or with the apostles' decision to lay hands on Matthias.

Scripture is clear that others besides the original eleven plus Paul functioned as apostles in taking oversight and appointing elders in the assemblies. The evidences of an apostle as stated by Paul (signs, wonders and miracles) were specially given to the original apostles and the other disciples in order to confirm the transition of God's authority from the Levitical priesthood of Israel to the Body of Christ from within all the nations. While Acts 15 indicates a distinction between the original twelve apostles and the elders, as well as the prophets, this is because the original apostles had a unique anointing that today's apostles do not have.

So the position of apostle in regards to the Body of Christ as a whole has not been operative since the first century. However, the position of the apostle for the local assembly is the anointing to go forth to establish other assemblies. Another function is that of offering apologetics for the Faith. There are still today true apostles who, although not possessing the same anointing as the first-century apostles, do rightly divide the Word of Truth and oversee the ministry of the local assembly—in some cases, several local assemblies. These would not be distinct from the other elders.

But just as there are true apostles, there are also false apostles who attempt to supplant or add to God's Word, exercising illegitimate power over any fellowships of which they can gain confidence. All aberrant "Christain" cult leaders are false apostles, as are those claiming that title in today's charismatic churches which are attempting to reestablish the doctrines of the Latter Rain Movement..

The true apostle will not allow those under his care to stray from the purity of God's Word. His authority is backed up by his ability to persuade the elders as a whole, and the assembly as a whole, not to follow false teachers and teachings that would subvert their faith.

In turn, the apostle is accountable to the assembly for his own adherence to Scripture. If he fails he is to be judged as a false apostle (Revelation 2:2):

> *Unto the angel of the assembly of Ephesus write; These things saith he that holdeth the seven stars in his right hand, who walketh in the midst of the seven golden candlesticks;*
>
> *I know thy works, and thy labour, and thy patience, and how thou canst not bear them which are evil: and thou hast tried them which say they are apostles, and are not, and hast found them liars:*
>
> *And hast borne, and hast patience, and for my name's sake hast laboured, and hast not fainted.*
>
> *Nevertheless I have somewhat against thee, because thou hast left thy first love.*
>
> *Remember therefore from whence thou art fallen, and repent, and do the first works; or else I will come unto thee quickly, and will remove thy candlestick out of his place, except thou repent.* (Revelation 2:1-5)

Some may argue that it is the angel or messenger to the assembly at Ephesus that is referred to as judging the false apostles. Yet every warning given to the messengers of all the seven assemblies in Asia is said to be what the Spirit is saying to the assemblies. When it comes to the faults cited, they are attributed to the assemblies, not to the angel or messenger to the assemblies.

Certainly all believers as priests of God have the Spirit of God to give them discernment, and the authority to make judgments based upon His Word. In any case, unless the false apostle repents, he—no less than anyone else in the assembly—is to be disfellowshipped.

Apostles today do not define the Faith which has been once and for all defined through the Scriptures. Nor are the signs of an apostle that Paul enumerated in 2 Corinthians 12:12 necessarily following today's apostles for several reasons:

- The original twelve were commissioned to establish the original assemblies; in practical terms, they operated in all the positions—apostles, prophets, evangelists, shepherds and teachers;

- The miracles they performed were part of that unique role, necessary to demonstrate to the people the transition of authority from the priests of Israel to the elders of the assemblies;

- There has been a lack of faith in the churches since the apostasy began in the third century;

- The churches are still largely apostate and lacking in proper leadership.

Today's apostles do not offer new revelations upon which the Faith is to be based and the believers to be held accountable. But they are true elders of the local assembly—those looked up to by the rest of the elders as having attained a status of honor due to their long service to the Lord and their faithfulness to His Word. They plant assemblies and oversee them until they come to maturity. They may or may not move on to plant other assemblies.

We should not be afraid of the word apostle merely because of the abuses committed by false apostles. The position is really not as imposing as some make it out to be. When the apostle's service is rendered in a spirit of humility and submission to the rest of the elders he is not to be feared, but honored.

As far as the number of apostles a fellowship should have, Scripture gives no indication. Let the Lord have His way and all things will be done decently and in order.

PROPHETS

When the term "prophet" is mentioned, there immediately springs to many minds the image of a bearded, sackcloth-clad person who proclaims doom and gloom upon those unheedful of his proclamations. The prophet who could call down fire from heaven or pronounce death or worse upon his adversaries is no longer among us. Today's prophet is one who calls the local body into accountability to God's Word. He does not prophesy new revelations that require the brethren's obedience.

The prophet has the gift of discernment to a large measure. He discerns error in teaching and practice and warns of the consequences if those espousing that error remain unrepentant.

Does God give revelation to His prophets, or are they to concern themselves only with discerning and speaking relative to Scripture? There is nothing in God's Word that would hinder a true prophet from receiving a word from the Lord warning of an impending crisis, or coming blessing for that matter. There are reports out of the underground assemblies in other countries where prophetic words warned of danger to the saving of many.

The reason we don't experience such things in the West to any great degree is that we largely don't believe in them. We don't need them; we're rich and increased in goods. Who needs God's prophets when "the Church" is so "holy"?

The true prophet is not a popular figure except among those who love God's Word without equivocation. That is, those who esteem Scripture as the only source of spiritual truth. Those who love true prophets hate human wisdom. Those called to task by the prophet for adding other "truths" to their teachings more often than not resist the prophet's appeals for repentance.

Today the prophet is not stoned for his audacity to hold church leadership accountable. Rather, he is politely neglected and/or spoken of in ridiculing terms. Most churches do not recognize their prophets as prophets, but as troublemakers who stir up the waters.

Women may function as prophetesses, because God's Spirit has been poured out upon all flesh (Acts 2:17). However, the position of prophet as one of the elders is reserved for men (1 Timothy 2:12).

Before rejecting difficult words, and dismissing the person who utters them, we'd best not forget Jesus' own testimony:

> ...*A prophet is not without honour, save in his own country, and in his own house.* (Matthew 13:57)

A truly biblical assembly holds its prophets in high regard while at the same time not neglecting to test the prophets by their own pronouncements.

In a sense, the apostle is a prophet to the elders, and the prophet is to hold the apostle, the elders and the congregation accountable to God's Word. At the same time, the prophet himself is subject to the apostles, the other elders and the congregation. All are to be subject to one another, which is the meaning of Ephesians 5:21.

Yet while we are all to be submitted to one another, there is special honor and recognition which should be given to those gifted with the positions of apostle and prophet.

EVANGELISTS

The word evangelist derives from the Greek *euaggelistou* (lit., "a messenger of good"). Other than Ephesians 4:11, which names evangelists among the elders of the assemblies, it is found only two times in Scripture. The first reference merely names Philip as an evangelist (Acts 21:8); the second is found in Paul's exhortation to Timothy to beware of false teachers and to do the work of an evangelist (2 Timothy 4:5).

With such limited reference to the position, it is left to the name itself to define the function of the evangelist, which traditionally is the proclaiming of the Gospel to nonbelievers.

An evangelist does not merely hold crusades in public arenas or proclaim the Gospel on street corners. Most evangelism is to individuals and small groups. This is far more effective and its results far more lasting than those of open air arenas.

This is not to dismiss the importance of public proclamations or mass meetings. The Holy Spirit has used men of God who have brought the Gospel to millions through this means. By the proclaiming of the Gospel by Peter more than 3,000 souls were added to the Body of Christ in one day (Acts 2:41).

To put things in perspective, every believer— man or woman—is supposed to evangelize. But although someone may be gifted with the ability to proclaim the Gospel publicly, the position of the evangelist in the assembly is reserved for men who meet the qualifications of an elder.

Therefore, the evangelists must be part of the governing body of the fellowship in order to bring their unique gift to bear for the edifying of the body and for the building up of the saints.

The evangelists function in the name of the assembly and bring order and substance to the proclaiming of the Gospel to non-believers brought into the assembly.

This does not mean that their testimony is limited to merely proclaiming Christ crucified and resurrected. In keeping with the Lord's admonition to count the cost before choosing to follow Him, evangelism must of necessity include a delineation of what God expects of those who trust in Him. They must be informed about counting the cost before making a decision to follow Jesus.

The evangelist must take personal responsibility for those to whom he has witnessed. Sometimes that may not be possible, such as was the case with Philip and the Ethiopian eunuch (Acts 8:27-39). In such cases the evangelist must commend those souls to God and trust Him to complete His work in them. But at the least, he should insist that converts under his ministry be baptized and submit themselves to the elders of a legitimate assembly, joining themselves in fellowship with the saints.

The practice of merely proclaiming the Gospel and then moving on, or of referring people to any church that will take them, has proven largely futile. Many new converts are left to flounder and/or to wind up in apostate churches. Some who claim the position of evangelist today even send converts into Roman Catholicism.

The evangelist must also stress water baptism by immersion as the means instituted by the Lord to wash away sins when coupled with faith in His atoning work on the cross. Too often baptism is relegated to mere ritual which may or may not be necessary.

The act of baptism does not save, but refusal to be baptized indicates lack of saving faith, provided the convert is correctly apprised of the need to be baptized according to God's Word.

Baptism is a command of the Lord. And if Peter names baptism as necessary to show repentance and confession of Christ before men, then the command must be obeyed.

Then Peter said unto them, Repent, and be baptized every one of you in the name of Jesus Christ for the remission of sins, and ye shall receive the gift of the Holy Ghost. (Acts 2:38)

The subject of baptism is dealt with in more detail in Appendix A. The important thing for evangelists to know is that, as a command of the Lord (Mark 16:16), baptism must follow the proclaiming of the full Gospel. It cannot be ignored as so often has been the case.

The evangelist does not generally go out on his own, but is sent by the local assembly with its blessing and covering. When sent out he should be supported by the fellowship so that nothing he requires is lacking. Wages lost through time taken from work should be made up by the assembly so that his family lacks nothing.

TEACHERS

It is often stated that the reference to pastors (shepherds) and teachers in Ephesians 14:11 implies that this is really one position combining the duties of pastor and teacher. This is only partly true, for Scripture tells us that all elders must be able to teach. Since shepherds are elders, they must also be able to teach; but so, too, must the apostles, the prophets and the evangelists, since they also comprise the eldership of the assembly.

To some degree all of the gifts will overlap among the elders as well as among the congregation.

That there were men spoken of as "teachers" without reference to shepherds indicates that the position of teacher is a separate anointing:

> *Now there were in the assembly that was at Antioch certain prophets and teachers; as Barnabas, and Simeon that was called Niger, and Lucius of Cyrene, and Manaen, which had been brought up with Herod the tetrarch, and Saul.*
>
> *As they ministered to the Lord, and fasted, the Holy Ghost said, Separate me Barnabas and Saul for the work whereunto I have called them.*
>
> *And when they had fasted and prayed, and laid their hands on them, they sent them away.* (Acts 13:1-3)

It seems that Paul was not speaking of a single position of shepherd-teacher in Ephesians 4:11, but was delineating two specific positions—those of a shepherd and of a teacher.

There are men who qualify as elders in every respect, but they are not gifted as apostles, prophets, evangelists or shepherds. These teachers minister the word as a gift in itself. They have the ability to rightly divide the Scriptures, and to relate the truth to the people in a way that touches their spirits, not just their ears.

However, all elders must be allowed to teach, for that is one of the qualifications for their position.

There is also a proper place for women to be able to teach:

> *The aged women likewise, that they be in behaviour as becometh holiness, not false accusers, not given to much wine, teachers of good things;*
>
> *That they may teach the young women to be sober, to love their husbands, to love their children,*
>
> *To be discreet, chaste, keepers at home, good, obedient to their own husbands, that the word of God be not blasphemed.* (Titus 2:3-5)

This is the only Scripture that speaks of women as teachers. The rule of the assembly is that the elders are to teach the men God's Word; the men, in turn, are to teach their wives and children. However, it is the example and the teaching by the elder women that show the younger women how to honor their husbands.

It is not really expedient for a man to teach his wife how and why she is to be in submission to him. It is far better if the elder women practiced this rule as an example and taught it to the younger women. This is not a formal type of teaching in an asssembly, but consistent teaching to one or a few.

Beyond this, teaching in the Body of Christ is reserved for the elders, and these are men only.

The rules for women are spelled out in 1 Timothy 2:9-15 and elsewhere in Scripture. Those who insist that women be given equal authority to teach and rule in the assembly are acting contrary to God's clearly stated instructions. The words of Paul are the words of Jesus, given through inspiration of the Holy Spirit.

SHEPHERDS

The scriptural word translated pastor from the Greek is *poimen* ("a shepherd, one who tends herds or flocks"). Only in Ephesians 4:11 is it rendered as "pastor" in the King James Bible. All other post-messianic scriptural references (17 in all) are rendered "shepherd" or "shepherds," and refer to Christ as the Shepherd of our souls, or to actual shepherds of sheep, or are metaphors in Christ's teachings for keepers of God's flock.

I prefer to call the true shepherds by that title rather than "pastor" in order to distinguish between them and those who rule in the clergy-laity-oriented churches.

Also, I purposely reversed the order of shepherds and teachers as outlined in Ephesians 14:11. My reason for doing so is that today's church pastors take to themselves the roles of shepherd and teacher as well as those of all the other positions. So I felt it would be more expedient to deal with it last.

Interestingly, the Ephesians 4:11 reference to shepherds is the only one in Scripture that applies to a position in the assembly. For having become the only position of any real authority in most churches, this is surprising and not a just a bit disconcerting. Scripture places less emphasis upon shepherds than upon the other positions which are mentioned several times.

Over the centuries, mainly due to the influence of Roman Catholicism, the position of shepherd has taken on a connotation that was never intended: a primary ruler—called "pastor"—of a synagogue, or teaching center, to whom all others are in subjection. This is also the role of the rabbi in Judaism, which may have played a role in the early Judaizers' influence in the churches. Even in churches where elders are more than a rubber stamp for the pastor's vision—where pastors are ostensibly in submission to an "elder board"—the reality is that the pastor fulfills virtually all the positions that Ephesians 4:11 enumerates.

Yet while the position of shepherd is never elaborated upon, the meaning is clear. A shepherd is one who tends the flock of God. He doesn't merely feed the flock as any hireling can do. Rather his primary responsibility is to guard it against spiritual danger and to lead it into pastures of truth. The shepherd's heart is to be one of gentleness and kindness, yet bold in admonishing those who are straying to remain in the Faith.

The shepherd binds the wounds of the flock and carries those he must to safety. If one strays, his heart goes out to the lost sheep and he will search for him until he has found him and brought him back into the fold. He visits the sick and those suffering in other ways. One who does not do these things is not a shepherd, no matter what his position is traditionally called.

More than one shepherd is needed in most fellowships, for the work required is often tiring and burdensome.

As with all the other positions, that of the shepherd finds similarity in the gifting of others in the assembly. Elder women may shepherd the younger women; other men may shepherd one another; even young people may shepherd other young people to some degree. But the position of the shepherd, like all the other positions, is reserved for men who possess the qualifications of elders.

So sacred is the position of the shepherd of God's flock that He has severe warnings for those who would abuse it (Jeremiah 2:8; 10:21; 12:10; 22:22; 23:1-2; Ezekiel 34:1-10). Although these words applied to the shepherds of Israel, they are no less spoken to anyone today who would assume such a sacred trust. It is especially sobering to realize that this sacred trust is representative of the Lord Himself. Throughout the Scriptures He is represented as the good and faithful Shepherd who loves and cares for His flock.

The shepherd's ministry is really to individuals more so than to the assembly as a whole. Some deacons may actually assume the role of shepherds to some degree.

DEACONS

There is another class of leaders who oversee the temporal needs of the congregation. These are called deacons (from the Greek, *diakonos*, which denotes an attendant, or waiter at tables or in other menial duties). This word is variously translated "servant," "minister," and, in the case of a position within the assembly, "deacon."

Women are also referred to in their role as servants, but not in relation to the position of a deacon, who must be the husband of one wife (it does not say, "the wife of one husband").

In his salutation to the Philippians, Paul alludes to a distinction between the elders and deacons:

> *Paul and Timotheus, the servants of Jesus Christ, to all the saints in Christ Jesus which are at Philippi, with the elders and deacons.* (Philippians 1:1)

This does not mean deacons are to be held in any less esteem than the elders in the assembly. The elders are the teaching and shepherding leaders. The deacons are men of equal spiritual maturity who serve the temporal needs of the flock.

The requirements for elders are strict, but no more strict than those for deacons, save for the ability to teach:

> *Likewise must the deacons be grave, not doubletongued, not given to much wine, not greedy of filthy lucre;*
>
> *Holding the mystery of the faith in a pure conscience.*
>
> *And let these also first be proved; then let them use the position of a deacon, being found blameless.*
>
> *Even so must their wives be grave, not slanderers, sober, faithful in all things.*
>
> *Let the deacons be the husbands of one wife, ruling their children and their own houses well.*
>
> *For they that have used the position of a deacon well purchase to themselves a good degree, and great boldness in the faith which is in Christ Jesus.* (1 Timothy 3:8-13)

The deacons must meet all the qualifications that the elders must meet. In a sense, the deacons are really non-teaching elders. For they, too, do the work of the ministry and edify the Body of Christ, working for the perfection of the saints (Ephesians 4:12).

The only real difference between the elders and the deacons is that the elders must be able to teach God's Word in the assembly. Also, the deacons are not spoken of as overseers of the flock in the way elders are. Yet due to their qualifications they should be afforded the same honor as the elders.

All who hold positions of authority in the local assembly comprise the leadership, whether elders (teaching leaders) or deacons (non-teaching leaders). Even deacons should have great boldness in the Faith to proclaim the Gospel.

*   *   *

What is written herein is difficult to ascertain and to put into practice. There are many pitfalls awaiting those who would assume leadership within the Body of Christ. Temptations of pride, to lord it over the people, to use one's position for personal gain and/or prestige—these and many other dangers await those who lead God's people.

There are dangers for the people as well. Pride may interfere with one's service to the Body of Christ under the direction of others. Many people don't like to submit to authority no matter how godly. The consequences for rebellion are grave.

Regarding the duties and responsibilities of the leaders, the Scriptures say little other than that those who rule must do so with humility and from a heart of love for God and for His people. In a sense, all leaders within the assembly assume the role of shepherd, for all must have the heart of a faithful shepherd.

The desire for financial support should not even be a consideration for those who would lead in the assembly. All must be willing to give sacrificially for the sake of the brethren. The brethren should be willing to give sacrificially for the sake of each other and for the elders. But no one should put a burden on others, or require that others give out of compulsion.

For those just beginning a new fellowship, it will be difficult to assess one another's spiritual qualities. It will be difficult not to want your own way in how things should be set up and how they should be run.

Who are the apostles?

Who are the prophets?

Who are the evangelists, the shepherds, the teachers, the deacons?

Rather than fret over these things, the first order of business must be prayer—diligent prayer that the Holy Spirit will lead in establishing a fellowship that will truly reflect the heart of God among His people.

But prayer isn't enough. We must also guard our hearts against temptation. We must put our love for the world and all of its enticements behind us. Purity of life is a prerequisite.

We must desire more than just getting together to discuss our likemindedness of opposition to the errors of "churchianity." This is very important: if any have been wounded by church leadership they must forgive. They must not harp on the injustices done to them. Feelings of anger, indignation, self-righteousness or smugness must not be allowed to hamper our ability to minister. If it is necessary to discuss these things, we must guard our hearts lest we fall into temptation and a snare that leads to bitterness. Be ready also to correct others if you detect these things in them. If we are faithful in these things, as time passes the men will sense the Lord's leading in recognizing the positions of those anointed by Him. In a sense, we are starting from scratch. We must work with what we have, and be led by the Word of God and His Spirit. There is no line of apostolic succession for the ordaining of elders, such as is claimed by Roman Catholicism and other aberrant Christian cults.

Every cult claims apostolic authority as the only true manifestation of God's Church upon the earth. They cannot all be right. In truth, none of them are right.

The Mormons, the Jehovah's Witnesses and many others claim that their leaders are the apostles of Christ. The Catholic Church claims that the pope is the successor to Peter and points to its existence from the first century. But the *ekklesia* in Rome to whom Paul wrote was not the Roman Catholic Church.

From the beginning, the Lord's apostles warned that the apostasy was already at work to destroy the Body of Christ (2 Thessalonians 2:7).

Paul warned the elders at Ephesus that grievous wolves would arise from among their own number:

> *Take heed therefore unto yourselves, and to all the flock, over the which the Holy Ghost hath made you overseers, to feed the church of God, which he hath purchased with his own blood.*
>
> *For I know this, that after my departing shall grievous wolves enter in among you, not sparing the flock.*
>
> *Also of your own selves shall men arise, speaking perverse things, to draw away disciples after them.*
>
> *Therefore watch, and remember, that by the space of three years I ceased not to warn every one night and day with tears.* (Acts 20:28-31)

What does this mean but that even the elders themselves could betray the flock. But this doesn't mean that God abandoned His people; He has allowed deception to exist in order to test our hearts.

Given these conditions, we must admit that, although God's people have existed as a remnant of the true Body of Christ through the centuries, they have largely been without proper leadership. Some have functioned as best they could under the present system that is far from perfect. But God is able to preserve His people in spite of ignorance, foolishness and lack of direction.

For centuries even the Scriptures were withheld from the people. With the Reformation came some enlightenment about God's grace, followed by the translation of the Bible into German, English and other languages.

Over the centuries God has been restoring previously lost truth. Why this has been necessary I cannot explain. All I know is that the churches have not functioned fully in accord with Scripture since the first or second century. This isn't to say that there has not been a remnant of believers who did not succumb to the apostasy, but visibly the churches have been largely apostate.

Yet the true Faith has survived until now. As we see the signs of the end of this age increasing, God is calling His people out from among the apostate churches into a new walk that is not new, but what has always been intended for His people.

Yes, every cult established since the Reformation has claimed to be the "restoration" of "the Church." Among leaders in the charismatic churches today there is the claim of "restoration." The problem is that they all want to be the leaders of that restoration, and they want their leadership to extend over all the churches.

They have only a small particle of truth. God indeed has been restoring His truth to His people since the time of the Reformation. But we are merely in the final stage (or one of the final stages) of that restoration. It has come line upon line, precept upon precept—here a little, there a little (Isaiah 28:10). When the restoration is complete it will not be through a universal "Church" leadership, but through the functioning of local, autonomous assemblies in the full manifestation of their ministries under the leadership of humble men.

Those involved in this restoration must take care not to establish another hierarchy or "movement." This has been the failing of the cults. Nor should it be something so complex that the average believer cannot function in his gifts.

With this restoration will come an accountability to God's Word and to other true brethren that has not been seen under the hierarchical structure for all these centuries. Each assembly will be autonomous, but each will hold others accountable should they stray from the truth. Not only will individuals be submitted to one another, assemblies will be submitted to one another. I firmly believe that the elders of one assembly will hold the elders of another assembly to accountability based upon God's Word, not upon denominational by-laws, charters and political-correctness. This should not interfere with each assembly's autonomy, for their authority will be Scripture, not some hierarchy.

In view of the current move away from establishment religion falsely called Christianity, the best we can do as we attempt to establish godly fellowship is to trust that God will do what He intends to do. As far as elders go, it would be best to at first just meet together for prayer and fellowship. Eventually, the elders will be manifested in your midst. Not because some will be more vocal than others, but because some will demonstrate the qualities of an elder and the humility necessary for that position. Their particular giftings will be manifested as well, whether as apostles, prophets, evangelists, shepherds, teachers or deacons.

It seems logical as well as scriptural that the first giftings to manifest themselves would be those of apostles and prophets. These would give assent to those who would hold the other positions.

While the congregation might choose godly men, full of the Holy Spirit, as did the believers in Jerusalem, ideally there should still be apostles to lay hands on them and appoint them for their position. There is no other scriptural method than that the apostles choose or at least confirm the choices of the assembly for elders.

One area of caution: often women tend to assert themselves within the assemblies. This must be tactfully prevented from the beginning. They must not be allowed to hold sway over the assembly. In fact, only the men in the assembly should appoint the elders. Otherwise, the women would have taken authority over the elders to begin with.

Do not try to rush things. Allow God to do what He will in His time. He has allowed us to come to this point over many centuries; He is quite capable of doing what must be done when necessary. A period of transition is not bad; it is a time to prepare our hearts for what God will be doing in our midst. Patience will be one of the most important attributes for those seeking to return to the first-century model for the assembly.

Based upon the Scriptures cited throughout this writing, an outline of the elders' qualifications and duties follows:

- They must be men;

- They must adhere to sound doctrine;

- They must be obedient to the Word of God;

- They must be humble;

- They must be sober;

- They must be kind;

- They must be bold in proclaiming truth and in holding the assembly to the authority of God's Word;

- They must labor without thought of financial reward;

- They must not show favoritism to those who give above those who do not give. (Nor should they show favoritism to the poor over the wealthy);

- They must hold their children in subjection to God's Word;

- Their wives must be humble and of gentle spirit lest they bring a disgrace upon their husbands, and thus upon the Body of Christ;

- They must be well thought of by unbelievers, notwithstanding that some unbelievers will never think well of believers in Jesus, and may even persecute them. But generally, unbelievers will respect the godly man;

- They must work outside the ministry to provide for their families (this is a general rule that may be adhered to in varying degrees, according to the leading of the assembly as a whole);

- They must submit to the other elders;

- They must submit their teachings to the scrutiny of the assembly as a whole;

- They must discharge the duties of their particular position with diligence, yet not infringe upon the duties of the other elders.

If a man is truly humble before God and before men, all these things and more will be normal for him. He will recognize whether or not he is even qualified to be an elder and, if not, will refuse the position. But he will also be obedient enough to accept if qualified.

Those who reject the biblical guidelines must be taught to conform or leave. As hard as that sounds, it is necessary in order for the assembly to function properly. Otherwise it will never come to the place of maturity that God requires.

6
Guidelines for Fellowship

When we speak of guidelines for fellowship, we are not speaking of ritual or how to construct a church service. We are speaking of rules that guide individual believers in relationship to one another, particularly when they come together for worship, prayer and ministry. As well, we should be aware of what the Lord requires in all our dealings with one another. Although Scripture is very clear in many areas, it seems as if even those clear teachings are largely ignored, or forgotten altogether. This is especially true in fellowships where the leadership's focus is on the teaching or preaching ministry and not sufficiently on the personal relationships within the fellowship. Often leadership is detached from the "average" believer. It is not unusual for pastors to limit their personal attention to those in leadership while largely ignoring the brethren at large. Elders often congregate together and neglect those they are to be shepherding. The only contact they may have with those under their care is in counseling sessions or in overseeing their church service. There is a disparity of ministry that often favors the "lovely" and neglects or avoids the "unlovely."

If I may be so bold, I suggest that a certain snobbishness exists within the Christian community. Just as in the world, the fellowship of many in the churches is not based on spiritual unity but on carnal factors. Likemindedness is paramount in the areas of commerce, sports, entertainment and other worldly pleasures or pursuits more so than in spiritual matters.

Those who are not as "sophisticated" as others are often left on the fringes not only of social gatherings but of ministry as well. Due to the nature of church leaders to incline toward intellectualism—or at least toward specific ways of thinking—those who do not measure up intellectually are more often tolerated than ministered to.

By the same token, those who are not of lovely face and form are shunned, if not for purposes of being ministered to, then for purposes of ministering. Good looks and natural talent too often take precedence over spiritual qualities. Churches wish to present the best visual and audio image. I am not suggesting that just anyone should be chosen to screech a solo "joyous noise" unto the Lord. But God's Word tells us that He chooses the poor and unseemly in this world over the rich and famous:

> For ye see your calling, brethren, how that not many wise men after the flesh, not many mighty, not many noble, are called:
> But God hath chosen the foolish things of the world to confound the wise; and God hath chosen the weak things of the world to confound the things which are mighty;
> And base things of the world, and things which are despised, hath God chosen, yea, and things which are not, to bring to nought things that are:
> That no flesh should glory in his presence.
> But of him are ye in Christ Jesus, who of God is made unto us wisdom, and righteousness, and sanctification, and redemption:
> That, according as it is written, He that glorieth, let him glory in the Lord. (1 Corinthians 1:26-31)

The reason God chooses those less capable is to demonstrate His own glory through them. He doesn't want us glorying in our natural abilities. As He says through Paul:

And these things, brethren, I have in a figure transferred to myself and to Apollos for your sakes; that ye might learn in us not to think of men above that which is written, that no one of you be puffed up for one against another.

For who maketh thee to differ from another? and what hast thou that thou didst not receive? now if thou didst receive it, why dost thou glory, as if thou hadst not received it? (1 Corinthians 4:6-7)

Not only do men act as if they have some virtue within themselves, they act as if they have some virtue apart from God's grace and gifting. They mistake knowledge of the Word and a natural ability to teach—along with a zeal to teach—as evidence that the Holy Spirit has gifted them to teach. Yet more often than not, the Holy Spirit works through those who are less talented and who would shun the spotlight. It is only after much agonizing over the true calling of God that many are equipped to teach or minister in any area. God help those who think that just because they **want** to serve God they **are equipped** to serve Him.

I recall many years ago, having just renewed my commitment to Christ, how zealous I was to be used by Him. Daily I prayed, "Lord, use me; Lord, use me." I had just prayed this same thing one evening while listening to a radio program called *Night Sounds*, hosted by Bill Pierce. As the beautiful music that interspersed Bill's biblical wisdom faded at one point, the first words he uttered were: "Many people pray, 'Lord, use me,' when they should be praying, 'Lord, make me usable.'"

In that instant I realized that, although I had knowledge, and was zealous to be used by God, I wasn't usable. I hadn't really surrendered all to Christ.

To surrender all means to surrender our very desire to serve Him. It means to be content where we are and allow Him to bring us to the place where He can use us to the fullest. It is only when the Holy Spirit is manifested in our service to Him through humility and genuine love of the brethren that He will be glorified.

Because we are led by our flesh in judging people's callings, we often fail to realize that God works through those whom we discern as less than favorable. As a result we miss out on blessings that accompany their presence.

This is a sin that plagues the churches, and yet is so subtle that it goes virtually undetected. The Scriptures that deal with this sin are overlooked in the process of ferreting out "deeper" truths. While engorging ourselves on those "deeper truths," we miss the fundamental requirement for functioning within the Body of Christ:

> *Owe no man any thing, but to love one another:*
> *for he that loveth another hath fulfilled the law.*
> (Romans 13:8)

Christians often mistake for love their own beneficent acts of kindness toward the poor. By putting canned goods and used clothing in the church's larder for distribution to the needy they believe they are fulfilling the law of love. While this may be a good work, it does not take the place of fellowship with those they would just as well prefer not to have any contact with on a personal level.

I recognize that it is impossible to have personal fellowship with everybody in the Body of Christ. But that is not the issue; the issue is **purposeful avoidance** of fellowship with those deemed less than up to one's earthly standards.

Regardless of those with whom we fellowship, there are rules set forth in Scripture which suggest more than just optional acquiescence. These rules are not to be sidestepped if the fellowship is to fulfill the purposes to which it has been called by God.

BE HUMBLE OF SPIRIT

One rule of fellowship is that we not think of ourselves as better than others. Man is naturally inclined toward comparing himself with others, either judging himself as greater or lesser based on righteousness, talents, intellect, or on any number of factors. What escapes him, unless confronted by God's Word, is that all have sinned and fallen short of the glory of God; no one is righteous compared to God, or worthy of merit before God:

As it is written, There is none righteous, no, not one:

There is none that under standeth, there is none that seeketh after God.

They are all gone out of the way, they are together become unprofitable; there is none that doeth good, no, not one. (Romans 3:10-12)

For all have sinned, and come short of the glory of God. (Romans 3:23)

When men compare themselves to other men they generally focus on those who are less endowed with whatever attributes they themselves possess. Thus, they become prideful:

For if any be a hearer of the word, and not a doer, he is like unto a man beholding his natural face in a glass:

For he beholdeth himself, and goeth his way, and straightway forgetteth what manner of man he was. (James 1:23-24)

We should compare ourselves to Jesus, not to other men:

Take my yoke upon you, and learn of me; for I am meek and lowly in heart: and ye shall find rest unto your souls. (Matthew 11:29)

Jesus is our example of humility; yet we see by His life that humility does not mean a false piety and milquetoast demeanor. It means honest appraisal of self before God. When we can look at ourselves in the light of Christ, then we will look into the perfect law of love and see how far short we fall; we will be humbled to the point of despair, and will claim, as did the Apostle Paul, that we are the chief of sinners. Only when we come to that place will we be suitable for service to God and to man. Only then will we be able to live by the law of love which requires that we surrender our personal desires in order to meet the desires of others, provided we not violate Scripture in the process (Philippians 2:5-8).

Humility and love are virtually synonymous, for it is not possible for true love to be expressed without humility. Thus we should look after the welfare of others above our own welfare.

The law of love is contrary to human nature. Man is basically selfish in his heart; he fights for his own desires above the desires of others. And it doesn't matter how much he protests his love for others, his natural instinct is to look out for number one. Many people will make sacrifices for the sake of those they love, but God's law of love requires that we make those same sacrifices for all others, even our enemies. That law cannot be obeyed until we have first put on humility and have put off the desire for revenge.

This is really an emulation of what Jesus did for us on the cross:

> For when we were yet without strength, in due time Christ died for the ungodly.
>
> For scarcely for a righteous man will one die: yet peradventure for a good man some would even dare to die.
>
> But God commendeth his love toward us, in that, while we were yet sinners, Christ died for us. (Romans 5:6-8)

Admittedly, this is impossible for man. Who would lay down his life for someone who has offended him? But with God all things are possible. If we will walk in the Spirit we will not fulfill the lusts of the flesh to do those things that place our needs and wants above the needs and wants of others. And we will forgive those who trespass against us; we will not seek retribution or vengeance, but will seek their greater good. A true believer in the Lord Jesus Christ has the same desire that God has, not willing that any should perish but that all should come to repentance (2 Peter 3:9).

Especially in the Body of Christ we must not take retribution against one whom we believe has offended us. God's Word is clear that if we have anything against a brother we should go to him and ask that he make things right, not for our sakes, but for his:

Moreover if thy brother shall trespass against thee, go and tell him his fault between thee and him alone: if he shall hear thee, thou hast gained thy brother.

But if he will not hear thee, then take with thee one or two more, that in the mouth of two or three witnesses every word may be established.

And if he shall neglect to hear them, tell it unto the assembly: but if he neglect to hear the assembly, let him be unto thee as an heathen man and a publican.

Verily I say unto you, Whatsoever ye shall bind on earth shall be bound in heaven: and whatsoever ye shall loose on earth shall be loosed in heaven.

Again I say unto you, That if two of you shall agree on earth as touching any thing that they shall ask, it shall be done for them of my Father which is in heaven.

For where two or three are gathered together in my name, there am I in the midst of them.

Then came Peter to him, and said, Lord, how oft shall my brother sin against me, and I forgive him? till seven times?

Jesus saith unto him, I say not unto thee, Until seven times: but, Until seventy times seven. (Matthew 18:15-22)

At first glance it seems as if the Lord is giving conflicting commands. On one hand, Jesus tells us that if our brother does something to injure us personally, we are to confront him even to the point of taking him before the assembly if necessary. On the other hand, He commands us to forgive our brother seventy times seven, or 490 times. Obviously the number 490 is not an iron-clad rule; we are not free to withhold forgiveness the 491st time. Few, if any, will offend us so often in our lifetime, but we offend God thousands of times, and He is always ready to forgive if we confess our sins.

But would this rule on forgiveness not conflict with Jesus' words to consider that brother a heathen and a publican (verse 17) if he does not repent of his injury to us?

In the first case, it seems that Jesus is telling us to confront the brother in order to bring him to repentance. He is not suggesting that this is for our own good, but rather for the good of our brother. Verse 15 tells us that in doing so we will gain a brother if he hears us.

It is the man who will not submit to biblical correction, but becomes stiff-necked about our plea, who is demonstrating rebellion. The reason for taking others to him is to establish the truth. The man has the opportunity to state his side. If the matter is established in our favor by the witnesses (not our friends, but neutral brethren), and the man still refuses to hear us, then the assembly (preferably the elders) should hear the matter and make a determination. If they side with us after hearing the testimony, and command the man to repent and make restitution if needed, and he still refuses to do so, he is to be considered as a heathen, which implies disfellowshiping him.

In view of those Scriptures that command us to consider others above ourselves, we should be careful that our motive in confronting one who offends us is based on our love for him and a desire that he learn of his sin in order to repent of it. We want him to be in good standing with our heavenly Father. If we merely want to get even, then sin is at *our* door. Hopefully the elders will recognize that sin and will call upon *us* to repent.

If we have unknowingly offended a brother in Christ and he tells us of that offense, we must be open to judge our own hearts and allow the Holy Spirit to convict us of our sin. However, there are times when someone takes offense when no offense was committed. In such a case we may either acquiesce to the brother's feelings of offense and apologize (knowing full well that we are deferring to him for the sake of peace), or we may plead our case for the possibility of misunderstanding on his part.

In either case, if we submit to the judgment of the elders we must be willing to abide by that judgment. This is a good reason to make sure that the assembly to which we join ourselves has godly elders that are led by the Holy Spirit and not by personal favoritism.

BE THE SERVANT OF ALL

Godly humility is a prerequisite for all ministry in the Body of Christ. The meaning of the word "ministry" is service. In the assembly it is most often used to denote the service of the elders toward the body. That is, the elders and deacons, though rulers over the spiritual and temporal affairs of the brethren, are to look upon their work as service or ministry to the people.

Sometimes that service means strong confrontation against sin. It isn't for the minister's sake that this confrontation must take place, it is for the sake of the one being ministered to.

Although there are the "official" ministers—the apostles, prophets, evangelists, shepherds, teachers and deacons—the burden of ministry to at least some degree lies upon every member of the Body of Christ. This is what Paul was alluding to in his first epistle to the Corinthians:

> *Now there are diversities of gifts, but the same Spirit.*
>
> *And there are differences of administrations, but the same Lord.*
>
> *And there are diversities of operations, but it is the same God which worketh all in all.*
>
> *But the manifestation of the Spirit is given to every man to profit withal.*
>
> *For to one is given by the Spirit the word of wisdom; to another the word of knowledge by the same Spirit;*
>
> *To another faith by the same Spirit; to another the gifts of healing by the same Spirit;*
>
> *To another the working of miracles; to another prophecy; to another discerning of spirits; to another divers kinds of tongues; to another the interpretation of tongues:*
>
> *But all these worketh that one and the selfsame Spirit, dividing to every man severally as he will.*
>
> *For as the body is one, and hath many members, and all the members of that one body, being many, are one body: so also is Christ.*

For by one Spirit are we all baptized into one body, whether we be Jews or Gentiles, whether we be bond or free; and have been all made to drink into one Spirit.

For the body is not one member, but many.

If the foot shall say, Because I am not the hand, I am not of the body; is it therefore not of the body?

And if the ear shall say, Because I am not the eye, I am not of the body; is it therefore not of the body?

If the whole body were an eye, where were the hearing? If the whole were hearing, where were the smelling?

But now hath God set the members every one of them in the body, as it hath pleased him.

And if they were all one member, where were the body?

But now are they many members, yet but one body.

And the eye cannot say unto the hand, I have no need of thee: nor again the head to the feet, I have no need of you.

Nay, much more those members of the body, which seem to be more feeble, are necessary:

And those members of the body, which we think to be less honourable, upon these we bestow more abundant honour; and our uncomely parts have more abundant comeliness.

For our comely parts have no need: but God hath tempered the body together, having given more abundant honour to that part which lacked:

That there should be no schism in the body; but that the members should have the same care one for another.

And whether one member suffer, all the members suffer with it; or one member be honoured, all the members rejoice with it.

Now ye are the body of Christ, and members in particular.

And God hath set some in the assembly, first apostles, secondarily prophets, thirdly teachers, after that miracles, then gifts of healings, helps, governments, diversities of tongues.

Are all apostles? are all prophets? are all teachers? are all workers of miracles?

Have all the gifts of healing? do all speak with tongues? do all interpret?

But covet earnestly the best gifts: and yet shew I unto you a more excellent way. (1 Corinthians 12:4-31)

Every member of the Body of Christ has a function; no one can stand alone, or even above the others. This is why we not forsake gathering together (Hebrews 10:24-25).

The more excellent way, of course, is to love. Love cannot exist without expressing itself in service to whatever capacity the gifts of the Holy Spirit will allow. But even love cannot keep one from frustration if one attempts to serve beyond the gifts and calling of God. This is why humility must be integral to the equation. Service performed out of duty rather than out of love will eventually result in frustration and, sometimes, despair. We must be able to discern when God is telling us to cease, and we are beginning to act in the flesh rather than in the Spirit.

An example may be our desire to see all our brethren prosper financially. We may take extraordinary steps to give or to collect for a particular brother who is lacking. This is okay if we keep it in perspective with God's Word. Citing Jesus' words, some believe they are to give to everyone who asks of them:

Give to him that asketh thee, and from him that would borrow of thee turn not thou away. (Matthew 5:42)

However, the context is that we should give to our enemies as a demonstration of love:

Ye have heard that it hath been said, An eye for an eye, and a tooth for a tooth:

But I say unto you, That ye resist not evil: but whosoever shall smite thee on thy right cheek, turn to him the other also.

And if any man will sue thee at the law, and take away thy coat, let him have thy cloke also.

And whosoever shall compel thee to go a mile, go with him twain.

Give to him that asketh thee, and from him that would borrow of thee turn not thou away.

Ye have heard that it hath been said, Thou shalt love thy neighbour, and hate thine enemy.

But I say unto you, Love your enemies, bless them that curse you, do good to them that hate you, and pray for them which despitefully use you, and persecute you;

That ye may be the children of your Father which is in heaven: for he maketh his sun to rise on the evil and on the good, and sendeth rain on the just and on the unjust.

For if ye love them which love you, what reward have ye? do not even the publicans the same?

And if ye salute your brethren only, what do ye more than others? do not even the publicans so?

Be ye therefore perfect, even as your Father which is in heaven is perfect. (Matthew 5:38-48)

By giving liberally to our enemies we are demonstrating the love of God to them. Whether or not our giving changes their hearts toward God is out of our hands. Sometimes that giving may entrench them in their sin; that is up to God to deal with. This doesn't mean we should give a drunkard money to buy alcoholic beverages, for that would not demonstrate love. It means that in those areas where we may not have knowledge, we ask the Father that whatever we give will be used by Him for His glory. We trust God with the outcome.

The command to give liberally to our brethren in Christ is stated in 1 John 3:17-18:

Hereby perceive we the love of God, because he laid down his life for us: and we ought to lay down our lives for the brethren.

But whoso hath this world's good, and seeth his brother have need, and shutteth up his bowels of compassion from him, how dwelleth the love of God in him?

My little children, let us not love in word, neither in tongue; but in deed and in truth.

The general rule is that if we see a brother in need, we are not to wait to be asked for help; we should offer our help immediately. And we are to give generously as the Lord leads us. However, we are not to act in the flesh in our giving any more than in any other service to the brethren.

If a brother is lazy and will not provide for himself or for his family, we do him no good service to support his indigence. This is how God's Word sums it up:

For even when we were with you, this we commanded you, that if any would not work, neither should he eat.

For we hear that there are some which walk among you disorderly, working not at all, but are busybodies.

Now them that are such we command and exhort by our Lord Jesus Christ, that with quietness they work, and eat their own bread.

But ye, brethren, be not weary in well doing.

And if any man obey not our word by this epistle, note that man, and have no company with him, that he may be ashamed.

Yet count him not as an enemy, but admonish him as a brother. (2 Thessalonians 3:10-15)

In such a case, love commands that we not allow our brother to continue in his sin, but rather point it out to him so he will repent. It is imperative that we know the facts of any case in which we desire to serve.

If we truly love the brethren we will desire to serve them in some capacity. And the greater our love, the greater will be our desire to serve. This is why we are advised to covet earnestly the best gifts—those that edify others more than one's self, as demonstrated in the Lord's admonition to His disciples:

> *But Jesus called them to him, and saith unto them, Ye know that they which are accounted to rule over the Gentiles exercise lordship over them; and their great ones exercise authority upon them.*
>
> *But so shall it not be among you: but whosoever will be great among you, shall be your minister:*
>
> *And whosoever of you will be the chiefest, shall be servant of all.*
>
> *For even the Son of man came not to be ministered unto, but to minister, and to give his life a ransom for many.* (Mark 10:42-45)

The higher one goes in position of authority in the assembly, the more one is to serve the brethren. This leaves no room for hierarchical thinking, pomp and circumstance, religious garb and special titles. Let's forget the degreed letters after names except when attempting to influence godless people who may harbor respect for such titles. If we are all brothers, let's call one another by our names. We should not contribute to a religious person's high regard for himself among the brethren. Nor should he insist that we do so.

The reason for so much confusion and demonic manifestations disguising themselves as "new moves" of God, is that most Christians are self-centered. They want some experience that will validate their spirituality. It doesn't matter what the experience is. As long as it comes in the name of the Lord and gives them a buzz, that's all they want. In fact, that's what they clamor for. And the so-called "ministers" leading them are just as self-centered. They aren't interested in the spiritual well-being of the people as much as they are in the acclamation they receive for their efforts (not to mention the filthy lucre that comes their way).

BE KIND TO ALL

Love commands that we be kind to all. Our carelessness in how we treat others often goes undetected. A curt word here, a failure to consider another's feelings there. These can add up to the point where we may alienate brethren in Christ who are prone to be easily offended.

Along the lines of being kind to one another, there is a Scripture that is often misunderstood:

> *Be ye therefore followers of God, as dear children;*
> *And walk in love, as Christ also hath loved us, and hath given himself for us an offering and a sacrifice to God for a sweet-smelling savour.*
> *But fornication, and all uncleanness, or covetousness, let it not be once named among you, as becometh saints;*
> *Neither filthiness, nor foolish talking, nor jesting, which are not convenient: but rather giving of thanks.*
> (Ephesians 5:1-4)

We all appreciate humor. No doubt the apostles had their share of light moments. But Scripture cautions us against "jesting." This is stated within the context of walking in love toward one another. Walking in love prohibits fornication, filthiness of mind, covetousness, foolish language and jesting.

It is often assumed that "foolish talking" and "jesting" refer to dirty jokes and sexual innuendo. While these are part of the equation, such talk also applies to anything that is not edifying, particularly when uttered within the context of fellowship.

Given our propensity to jest with one another, we sometimes stray over the line of good taste and end up demeaning one another. We point out someone's faults in humorous tones, not realizing that we are holding him up to ridicule. Even when done in jest, unkind words can have devastating effects.

Such can be the result of too close a relationship, where we begin to take for granted that someone we put down will not, or should not, take offense because we assume that they know we love them.

Good-natured kidding may be okay up to a point. But put-downs are never kind. We must be careful not to speak in such a manner that it causes a brother or sister to take offense. To cross that boundary does not demonstrate love, but carelessness in our relationships.

Those who offend in this way risk losing the relationships they value. On the other hand, those who are offended by others' jesting should be ready to forgive and not take offense too easily. Just as we do not want others to expect perfection from us, we cannot expect perfection from them. However, we should strive to be perfect in our dealings with others. This doesn't mean we won't fail; it does mean that when we do fail we acknowledge that failure and ask forgiveness.

God's Word lists certain specifics related to kindness:

Let all bitterness, and wrath, and anger, and clamour, and evil speaking, be put away from you, with all malice:

And be ye kind one to another, tenderhearted, forgiving one another, even as God for Christ's sake hath forgiven you. (Ephesians 4:31-32)

Put on therefore, as the elect of God, holy and beloved, bowels of mercies, kindness, humbleness of mind, meekness, longsuffering;

Forbearing one another, and forgiving one another, if any man have a quarrel against any: even as Christ forgave you, so also do ye.

And above all these things put on charity, which is the bond of perfectness. (Colossians 3:12-14)

And beside this, giving all diligence, add to your faith virtue; and to virtue knowledge;

And to knowledge temperance; and to temperance patience; and to patience godliness;

And to godliness brotherly kindness; and to brotherly kindness charity.

For if these things be in you, and abound, they make you that ye shall neither be barren nor unfruitful in the knowledge of our Lord Jesus Christ.

But he that lacketh these things is blind, and cannot see afar off, and hath forgotten that he was purged from his old sins.

Wherefore the rather, brethren, give diligence to make your calling and election sure: for if ye do these things, ye shall never fall. (2 Peter 1:5-10)

Kindness is not an option; it is an essential aspect of fellowship. Kindness is manifested in works of charity; it is revealed in small acts of consideration and politeness. It is especially important that kindness be shown to the elderly and the infirm. And it must be demonstrated in all relationships with our brethren in Christ:

Rebuke not an elder, but intreat him as a father; and the younger men as brethren;
The elder women as mothers; the younger as sisters, with all purity. (1 Timothy 5:1-2)

How I wish I could take back the times that I have lacked such kindness in my relationships with others. How often young people fail to demonstrate kindness to their elders; they think they have greater wisdom than those who have gone before them; they consider them something to be mocked or, at best, tolerated. If they only knew how many of life's pitfalls could be avoided if they would only listen to their elders and treat them with the respect they deserve.

Kindness should be demonstrated as a matter of course. But there are different ways to show kindness, particularly where sin is concerned. In relation to men treating younger women as sisters, young people today fail to treat one another with respect and purity. The consequences are evident in the churches through abortions and illegitimate births.

There was a time when a birth out of wedlock brought shame to the churches. Now it is celebrated with the same fervor as births within marriage. The child is held up to the congregation's applause and showers are given for the mother. What message does this send to the young people in the assembly?

True love and kindness would forego these approaches to sin. While it is imperative that kindness be shown to the mother and child, the father should be brought before the elders and made aware of his duty to support the girl and the child, with the hope that he would comply. That would demonstrate love and kindness to all parties—not allowing any to escape the responsibilities of their actions. It would be kindness to the congregation—particularly the youth, by showing them that love is tied up in responsibility.

By all means, the mother and child should be given the help they may need, provided the mother has demonstrated repentance; but this should be done privately, without fanfare and ceremony.

This is only one example of exercising kindness within the biblical context. Such actions may seem contrary to kindness, but the intention is to help those in sin without scandalizing the Body of Christ.

Kindness emulates our heavenly Father who is kind to all:

> *But love ye your enemies, and do good, and lend, hoping for nothing again; and your reward shall be great, and ye shall be the children of the Highest: for he is kind unto the unthankful and to the evil.* (Luke 6:36)

God's kindness is reflected in His provision of Christ as a sacrifice for our sins:

> *But God, who is rich in mercy, for his great love wherewith he loved us,*
> *Even when we were dead in sins, hath quickened us together with Christ, (by grace ye are saved;)*
> *And hath raised us up together, and made us sit together in heavenly places in Christ Jesus:*
> *That in the ages to come he might shew the exceeding riches of his grace in his kindness toward us through Christ Jesus.*
> *For by grace are ye saved through faith; and that not of yourselves: it is the gift of God:*
> *Not of works, lest any man should boast.* (Ephesians 2:4-9)

> *But after that the kindness and love of God our Saviour toward man appeared,*

Not by works of righteousness which we have done,
but according to his mercy he saved us, by the washing
of regeneration, and renewing of the Holy Ghost;
Which he shed on us abundantly through Jesus
Christ our Saviour;
That being justified by his grace, we should be made
heirs according to the hope of eternal life. (Titus 3:4-7)

In exercising kindness we are demonstrating love and humility. And although often misunderstood, kindness is demonstrated in discipline and judgment where sin and false teaching is concerned—provided, of course, that our judgment is righteous judgment and not self-righteous judgment.

JUDGE RIGHTEOUSLY

A problem that is systemic in the churches is that of judging unrighteously. We all have some preconceived ideas of what constitutes right and wrong, not all of which are necessarily grounded in Scripture. Because our conscience is offended by something, we assume that everyone's conscience should be offended by that same thing as well.

I am not speaking of sin as delineated in Scripture, but of practices that may be deemed sinful by a religious establishment, by negative personal experiences or by plain human reasoning based on a religious or moral mindset.

The early assemblies were already beleaguered by legalists who imposed restrictions on food and drink as well as on other practices. Paul addresses these in Romans 14:

Him that is weak in the faith receive ye, but not to
doubtful disputations.
For one believeth that he may eat all things:
another, who is weak, eateth herbs.
Let not him that eateth despise him that eateth not;
and let not him which eateth not judge him that
eateth: for God hath received him.
Who art thou that judgest another man's servant?
to his own master he standeth or falleth. Yea, he shall
be holden up: for God is able to make him stand.

One man esteemeth one day above another: another esteemeth every day alike. Let every man be fully persuaded in his own mind.

He that regardeth the day, regardeth it unto the Lord; and he that regardeth not the day, to the Lord he doth not regard it. He that eateth, eateth to the Lord, for he giveth God thanks; and he that eateth not, to the Lord he eateth not, and giveth God thanks.

For none of us liveth to himself, and no man dieth to himself.

For whether we live, we live unto the Lord; and whether we die, we die unto the Lord: whether we live therefore, or die, we are the Lord's.

For to this end Christ both died, and rose, and revived, that he might be Lord both of the dead and living.

But why dost thou judge thy brother? or why dost thou set at nought thy brother? for we shall all stand before the judgment seat of Christ.

For it is written, As I live, saith the Lord, every knee shall bow to me, and every tongue shall confess to God.

So then every one of us shall give account of himself to God.

Let us not therefore judge one another any more: but judge this rather, that no man put a stumblingblock or an occasion to fall in his brother's way.

I know, and am persuaded by the Lord Jesus, that there is nothing unclean of itself: but to him that esteemeth any thing to be unclean, to him it is unclean.

But if thy brother be grieved with thy meat, now walkest thou not charitably. Destroy not him with thy meat, for whom Christ died.

Let not then your good be evil spoken of:

For the kingdom of God is not meat and drink; but righteousness, and peace, and joy in the Holy Ghost.

For he that in these things serveth Christ is acceptable to God, and approved of men.

Let us therefore follow after the things which make for peace, and things wherewith one may edify another. (Romans 14:1-19)

It is significant that these words were penned especially to the assemblies in Rome. In later times those assemblies became apostate and merged under a religious hierarchy which eventually became known as Roman Catholicism. That hierarchy began to impose dire condemnation upon people for eating certain things at certain times, for not observing special days in special ways, for not abstaining from meat, even forbidding its "priests" to marry. Judgment came through the hierarchy of that church and filtered down through its religious-minded adherents. And that same unrighteous judgment continues to this day.

Many Protestant churches have incorporated their own lists of taboos which are not supported by Scripture when rightly divided. Some, on the other hand, have thrown off even biblical restrictions in the name of freedom in Christ. Both approaches are wrong.

Just as God gave everything freely to Adam and Eve, yet forbade them to eat from one specific tree, so Christ has given us liberty in all things except those which His Word specifically forbids. Even so, we are commanded not to cause our brother to stumble on account of the biblical liberty that we possess.

We are to judge ourselves:

Wherefore whosoever shall eat this bread, and drink this cup of the Lord, unworthily, shall be guilty of the body and blood of the Lord.

But let a man examine himself, and so let him eat of that bread, and drink of that cup.

For he that eateth and drinketh unworthily, eateth and drinketh damnation to himself, not discerning the Lord's body.

For this cause many are weak and sickly among you, and many sleep.

> *For if we would judge ourselves, we should not be judged.*
>
> *But when we are judged, we are chastened of the Lord, that we should not be condemned with the world.* (1 Corinthians 11:27-32)

If we are to judge ourselves righteously, it is required that we view ourselves from the perspective of God's holiness. Here, again, Jesus is our only example.

We are to judge sin in our midst:

> *I wrote unto you in an epistle not to company with fornicators:*
>
> *Yet not altogether with the fornicators of this world, or with the covetous, or extortioners, or with idolaters; for then must ye needs go out of the world.*
>
> *But now I have written unto you not to keep company, if any man that is called a brother be a fornicator, or covetous, or an idolater, or a railer, or a drunkard, or an extortioner; with such an one no not to eat.*
>
> *For what have I to do to judge them also that are without? do not ye judge them that are within?*
>
> *But them that are without God judgeth. Therefore put away from among yourselves that wicked person.* (1 Corinthians 5:9-13)

By judging sin in the assembly we can help save the sinner:

> *Keep yourselves in the love of God, looking for the mercy of our Lord Jesus Christ unto eternal life.*
>
> *And of some have compassion, making a difference:*
>
> *And others save with fear, pulling them out of the fire; hating even the garment spotted by the flesh.* (Jude 1:21-23)

By judging sin in the assembly we can help prevent others from falling into sin:

Them that sin rebuke before all, that others also may fear. (1 Timothy 5:20)

This word from Paul to Timothy must not be taken to mean that just any individual can stand before the assembly and point out the sins of others. It was given to Timothy in his role as an apostle and evangelist—an elder in his assembly.

If one has knowledge of another's unrepentant sin, he should first confront the brother privately; if the brother does not repent, and especially if the sin is known generally in the assembly, one should then take the matter to the elders. The elders must then make a judgment based upon God's Word clearly stated. It is encumbent upon the one brought before the elders to honestly assess his condition. If he can make no scriptural defense, then he must acquiesce to the elders' decision. And here, as in all cases of confrontation, the motive must be for the sake of the sinner's benefit, not for the sake of self-righteousness.

We are to judge disputes in the Body of Christ

Dare any of you, having a matter against another, go to law before the unjust, and not before the saints?

Do ye not know that the saints shall judge the world? and if the world shall be judged by you, are ye unworthy to judge the smallest matters?

Know ye not that we shall judge angels? how much more things that pertain to this life?

If then ye have judgments of things pertaining to this life, set them to judge who are least esteemed in the ekklesia.

I speak to your shame. Is it so, that there is not a wise man among you? no, not one that shall be able to judge between his brethren?

But brother goeth to law with brother, and that before the unbelievers.

Now therefore there is utterly a fault among you, because ye go to law one with another. Why do ye not rather take wrong? why do ye not rather suffer yourselves to be defrauded?

> *Nay, ye do wrong, and defraud, and that your brethren.* (1 Corinthians 6:1-8)

The better way is not to sue a brother or even take him before the assembly unless the latter action may result in spiritual good for him. We must be willing to suffer loss rather than take our disputes before the world, thus scandalizing the name of Jesus before unbelievers. How often the Lord has been scandalized and the Body of Christ mocked because of financial schemes, injustices and lawsuits in the name of being a Christian.

Yet if we have been wronged by a brother in Christ, we have the means to settle the dispute: godly men in authority who can render a judgment which binds the litigants. Once brethren agree to abide by the decision of the elders, they must not fail to meet the terms of the judgment. To do so would bring worse penalties than any that man's judicial system can impose. Just because God doesn't render immediate justice for wrongdoing doesn't mean His final judgment will be lenient. Those who become stiffnecked against the judgments of God, or of any rightfully instituted human authority, or of godly spiritual authority, risk losing far more than they would ever lose in human society.

Before God, a council of elders formed to settle disputes is every bit a legal court of law as any in the world. If one refuses to enter into arbitration before the elders he must give up any claims; he is not free to go to court against a brother in Christ. He should suffer loss and make peace with his brother. God's Word indicates that this same principle applies toward our enemies.

> *If it be possible, as much as lieth in you, live peaceably with all men.*
>
> *Dearly beloved, avenge not yourselves, but rather give place unto wrath: for it is written, Vengeance is mine; I will repay, saith the Lord.*
>
> *Therefore if thine enemy hunger, feed him; if he thirst, give him drink: for in so doing thou shalt heap coals of fire on his head.*
>
> *Be not overcome of evil, but overcome evil with good.* (Romans 12:18-21)

This is the law of love. Seeing then that God does not want us to take revenge against those who injure us, yet allows us to take an offending brother before the assembly, it becomes clear by the law of love that our reason for bringing him before the assembly is to offer him a chance to repent for his own sake. However, we must be careful not to use this as a rationalization to get even. Only after much searching of our own hearts in the matter should we consider this course of action. But in no case are we allowed to sue a brother (or even one who claims to be a Christian) in a court of law. Better that we suffer loss than bring a reproach against the Lord's name.

If we have defrauded a brother in Christ, or anyone else for that matter, we should not wait until we have been confronted to make things right. We should make amends immediately.

Even if we have been an innocent party to a brother's loss we should make amends.

One example would be taking a brother into a commercial enterprise that results in his being injured financially. We may well believe that that "limited partnership" or other deal will result in profit to him. But if he ventures into it based on his trust in us, we are bound to do what we can to see that he doesn't suffer loss. We may not be able to make restitution immediately, but we should seek his forgiveness and attempt to pay him back as best we can.

This should be a lesson to those who think that their standing in the fellowship entitles them to the trust of others in financial dealings, especially if their standing is that of a pastor. Many pastors have entered into get-rich quick schemes, multi-level-marketing endeavors and other money-making enterprises, hoping to cash in on their congregation's participation. Every one I've ever heard about has resulted in loss not only to the naïve pastor, but to the congregation as well. By using spiritual fellowship for the purpose of monetary gain they violate God's Word and ignore His warning:

> *But they that will be rich fall into temptation and a snare, and into many foolish and hurtful lusts, which drown men in destruction and perdition.*

> *For the love of money is the root of all evil: which while some coveted after, they have erred from the faith, and pierced themselves through with many sorrows.*
>
> *But thou, O man of God, flee these things; and follow after righteousness, godliness, faith, love, patience, meekness.* (1 Timothy 6:9-11)

How much better things would be if financial dealings were not part of Christian fellowship. Mammon (the love of money) has probably caused more problems in the Body of Christ than any other single thing, with the possible exception of fornication. If we would avoid mixing business with the Faith we would avoid having to enter into judgment in many instances.

In the case where we may sit in judgment in a dispute, we are commanded not to show partiality to the rich or to the poor; we are to judge righteously:

> *Ye shall do no unrighteousness in judgment: thou shalt not respect the person of the poor, nor honour the person of the mighty: but in righteousness shalt thou judge thy neighbour.* (Leviticus 19:15)

To show partiality to the poor out of compassion is to rob another in the name of God. Nor is compromise the objective; justice must be the objective.

The world always seeks compromise because it cannot abide absolute truth; it seeks to find a common ground of meeting so that no one is offended. But compromise robs the truth of its integrity and puts it on the same level with falsehood. This may be the world's way, but it is not God's way.

We are to judge those speaking in God's name:

> *Beloved, believe not every spirit, but try the spirits whether they are of God: because many false prophets are gone out into the world.* (1 John 4:1)
>
> *Let the prophets speak two or three, and let the other judge.* (1 Corinthians 14:29)

*Unto the angel of the assembly of Ephesus write;
These things saith he that holdeth the seven stars in his
right hand, who walketh in the midst of the seven
golden candlesticks;*

*I know thy works, and thy labour, and thy patience,
and how thou canst not bear them which are evil: and
thou hast tried them which say they are apostles, and are
not, and hast found them liars:*

*And hast borne, and hast patience, and for my
name's sake hast laboured, and hast not fainted.*
(Revelation 2:1-3)

*Now we have received, not the spirit of the world,
but the spirit which is of God; that we might know the
things that are freely given to us of God.*

*Which things also we speak, not in the words which
man's wisdom teacheth, but which the Holy Ghost
teacheth; comparing spiritual things with spiritual.*

*But the natural man receiveth not the things of the
Spirit of God: for they are foolishness unto him: neither
can he know them, because they are spiritually discerned.*

*But he that is spiritual judgeth all things, yet he
himself is judged of no man.*

*For who hath known the mind of the Lord, that he
may instruct him? But we have the mind of Christ.* (1
Corinthians 2:12-16)

One of the great sins of the modern churches is the refusal
to judge the teachings of others. This is a problem with the
church model wherein it is considered not only unloving to do
so, but impolite. Our "civilized" culture frowns on confrontation;
it makes people uncomfortable to hear others vociferously
contend for their beliefs. Whether those beliefs are right or
wrong isn't the issue; the issue is peace at any price.

As a result of this cultural proclivity toward politeness,
Christians sit in their pews listening to doctrines of demons and
watching demonic practices take place without challenge. A
pastor can spout the worst heresy and no one will call him to
account publicly because that would be impolite. And ushers

stand ready to physically remove anyone who would dare do so. Society propagates this cowardice by imposing penalties and fines for anyone who disrupts a religious service.

It may be well that government is ready to protect religions against undue harassment from those who are not of the particular religion in question, but it has no business entering into the disputes among those who claim to be of like faith, particularly if one disrupting the service is a member of the assembly. Religious leaders who would take advantage of such laws are demonstrating a lack of confidence in what they teach. If they cannot defend their teachings and practices to their congregants, but must use force to evict one who questions them on a reasonable and scriptural basis, they are unsuited for a defense of the Faith. As well, they are sinning by taking a brother before the secular courts to protect their religious "rights."

This doesn't mean, however, that just because a teacher misstates something apart from an obvious heresy we have the freedom to call him down in front of the assembly. It would be best to first confront him in private, try to reason with him from Scripture on the areas that need correction, and then ask him to make a public retraction of his error.

When we fail to judge false teachings we are not being loving; we are being cowardly. We are leaving the sheep to be devoured by the adversary. All believers in Christ assume the role of a watchman. We all have the Holy Spirit who gives us the ability to discern truth from error. If we fail to warn the brethren of the error in their midst we are guilty of that same error, even if we disagree with it.

> *Son of man, I have made thee a watchman unto the house of Israel: therefore hear the word at my mouth, and give them warning from me.*
>
> *When I say unto the wicked, Thou shalt surely die; and thou givest him not warning, nor speakest to warn the wicked from his wicked way, to save his life; the same wicked man shall die in his iniquity; but his blood will I require at thine hand.*

Yet if thou warn the wicked, and he turn not from his wickedness, nor from his wicked way, he shall die in his iniquity; but thou hast delivered thy soul.

Again, When a righteous man doth turn from his righteousness, and commit iniquity, and I lay a stumblingblock before him, he shall die: because thou hast not given him warning, he shall die in his sin, and his righteousness which he hath done shall not be remembered; but his blood will I require at thine hand.

Nevertheless if thou warn the righteous man, that the righteous sin not, and he doth not sin, he shall surely live, because he is warned; also thou hast delivered thy soul. (Ezekiel 3:17-21)

Those who have knowledge of evil but fail to warn the brethren are betraying them to the wolves to be devoured. This is especially true of the leaders within the assembly.

With all this, we must keep in mind the many Scriptures that warn against judging. All things must be in balance, based upon the Word of God and ministered by the Spirit of God. When we attempt to judge others by our own judgment we are guilty of hypocrisy.

THE STRONG TO BEAR THE WEAK

Immediately following his instructions on not judging according to what one eats or drinks, Paul instructs us that those who are strong in the faith must bear with the weaknesses of others who have not attained to the same spiritual maturity:

We then that are strong ought to bear the infirmities of the weak, and not to please ourselves.

Let every one of us please his neighbour for his good to edification.

For even Christ pleased not himself; but, as it is written, The reproaches of them that reproached thee fell on me.

For whatsoever things were written aforetime were written for our learning, that we through patience and comfort of the scriptures might have hope.

Now the God of patience and consolation grant you to be likeminded one toward another according to Christ Jesus:

That ye may with one mind and one mouth glorify God, even the Father of our Lord Jesus Christ.

Wherefore receive ye one another, as Christ also received us to the glory of God. (Romans 15:1-7)

We must please others before ourselves when it comes to unimportant aspects of living. Even though we have freedom in Christ we should restrict ourselves in what we eat and drink so that we not offend our brother or cause him to stumble. Too often Christians assert their "right" to do as they please, without regard to the feelings of those who may (rightly or wrongly) perceive those actions as sinful, or at least undesirable. So while taking advantage of their liberty they are breaking the law of love which supersedes all other considerations. Not allowing themselves to be judged by men on what they eat or drink, they open themselves up for judgment by God on their lack of love.

At the same time we refuse the judgment of others, we willingly judge them for what we perceive as sin. In either case, even when judging sin as defined by Scripture, we must first judge ourselves. This is what Jesus meant when He commanded us to "Judge not according to the appearance, but judge righteous judgment" (John 7:24).

There is a righteous judgment which cannot be challenged because it is predicated upon God's truth as revealed in His Word. It is not predicated upon man's religious ideas and personal likes and dislikes. Yet even when exercising such righteous judgment we must be careful that we are not being hypocritical:

Judge not, that ye be not judged.

For with what judgment ye judge, ye shall be judged: and with what measure ye mete, it shall be measured to you again.

And why beholdest thou the mote that is in thy brother's eye, but considerest not the beam that is in thine own eye?

Or how wilt thou say to thy brother, Let me pull out the mote out of thine eye; and, behold, a beam is in thine own eye?

Thou hypocrite, first cast out the beam out of thine own eye; and then shalt thou see clearly. (Matthew 7:1-5)

In view of the many Scriptures that tell us to judge, it is obvious that the Lord is not telling us to refrain entirely from judging others. He is warning us that the same standard by which we judge others will be used against us when we are judged by God. It is a common practice that those who want license to do as they please will quote the first verse and ignore the preponderance of Scripture that requires them to judge sin in their midst. When taken in context we see that the Lord was warning us not to judge a brother who sins if we are in sin ourselves.

Obviously we will always be sinful as long as we are in this flesh, but a man's heart attitude toward his own sin must be one of revulsion and a desire to root it out of his life. As well, he must have confessed his sin to the Lord before confronting another brother for his sin. This is what Jesus meant when he said that we must first remove the beam out of our own eye before we can even confront a brother about the mote in his. When we do confront a brother in sin we must still exercise humility and mercy:

Be ye therefore merciful, as your Father also is merciful.

Judge not, and ye shall not be judged: condemn not, and ye shall not be condemned: forgive, and ye shall be forgiven. (Luke 6:36-37)

Our Father is immensely patient and merciful toward us; He requires that we be the same toward our brethren. Every avenue of escape must be presented to a brother in sin. The first avenue is confrontation. If we are not spiritually prepared to confront a brother in sin we are failing in our calling by the Lord; worse, we are failing our brother who needs our correction. It is a sad thing to see sin go unjudged in the Body of Christ because those in leadership are either spiritually deficient, or are too cowardly to address that sin. They would rather ignore sin for the sake of peace, thus bringing the leaven to full loaf.

In all cases of judgment we must focus on the real sin, not on the heart of the sinner. It is up to God to judge hearts:

> *Therefore judge nothing before the time, until the Lord come, who both will bring to light the hidden things of darkness, and will make manifest the counsels of the hearts: and then shall every man have praise of God.* (1 Corinthians 4:5)

MINISTRY TO YOUTH & CHILDREN

Much is said about fellowship among the brethren, that is, adults. But there is the aspect of adult-child relationships within the Body of Christ that needs to be addressed.

As a rule, today's churches provide separate ministry for children and young people. As soon as the family walks into the church building it fragments into peer groups. Ideally, children should be with their parents through at least part of the ministry, hearing the Word of God and worshiping together. There is room for children's ministry provided it does not become an end in itself or prevent children from experiencing the assembly in action.

Scripture does not deal with this issue because it didn't exist in the early assemblies. But because it isn't in Scripture doesn't mean it is totally invalid. If there is going to be any specific ministry to children it seems that biblical guidelines do exist.

Many, if not most, Sunday school teachers for children are women. They teach both boys and girls. This may be alright up to the point where a boy reaches puberty. But at that stage he is to be considered a man and his teachers should be men. We are not talking about emotional maturity, but physical maturity. Admittedly, this is my own reasoning from what I know of Scripture and Jewish tradition that would have prevailed for the early believers.

It is perfectly alright for women to teach young girls and other women, provided they focus on the areas that Scripture delineates:

> *The aged women likewise, that they be in behaviour as becometh holiness, not false accusers, not given to much wine, teachers of good things;*
> *That they may teach the young women to be sober, to love their husbands, to love their children,*
> *To be discreet, chaste, keepers at home, good, obedient to their own husbands, that the word of God be not blasphemed.* (Titus 2:3-5)

This is not a formal teaching, but an ongoing ministry of teaching and example in everyday life.

Today's feminist religious demands aside, God's primary purpose for women is to keep their home and raise their children in the love of the Lord. To do otherwise is to open God's Word to be blasphemed—broken by wilfull disobedience.

If young girls were taught this at an early age, and efforts were made to offset the messages to the contrary that they are receiving from the world, Christian marriages would be the envy of society.

So let the men teach the men as soon as they reach puberty; let the women teach the girls and young women to follow God's instructions for them, not to follow the contrary ways of the world.

Generally, all adults should treat children with love and kindness, and all children should treat adults with respect and honor. Regardless of how society does things, it is proper to have children call adults by Mr. and Mrs., rather than by first names. Familiarity for children in addressing adults is wrong. It is up to parents to teach their children that proper respect is also tied to the manner in which they address their elders.

Now, I'm going to say something that must be said at the risk of offending some of today's modern parents. For many, children are the center of their universe. While it is important for children to be cared for, when it comes to the assembling of the believers they must not be allowed to disrupt things. I've been in meetings where children have been allowed to run around, interrupt their parents and even the speaker, and generally take the people's attention from the Word of God.

The parents have sat mute while their children have wreaked havoc with the proceedings. This ought not to be. If the parents cannot control their children, then something is wrong with their parenting. The elders, and preferably other parents, should intervene and help the miscreant parents understand that the gathering of the saints is a sacred thing. Common courtesy should be expected there no less than in any other public setting.

Would they allow such behavior in a church? Of course not. Would they allow such behavior in a civil court, or government chambers? No, they should respect such institutions because they recognize their sanctity. All the more should they recognize and respect the greater sanctity of the Lord's assembly.

Should the child become so disruptive that it must be removed, then the mother should take that responsibility. It is not up to the father in this case because he is the one who should be learning the Word of God first, so he can teach his wife and children.

Those who think this is a "sexist" comment are infected with the world's values and must be taught that God's ways are not man's ways. He has established the rules for the family, and commands that children must obey and honor their parents. It is not up to the parents to acquiesce to their children's desires. By the same token, the wife is not the one to be learning the Word apart from her husband unless he is not able to be present.

For the very young it would be advantageous if the mothers in the assembly took turns caring for them in another room until they reach the age when they can understand what is going on, or at least be able to maintain some decorum so as not to disrupt the assembly.

There is no place for "peer" groups for children. They would be far better off listening to the adults share the Word than in some separate meeting that caters to their adolescent or pre-adolescent nature. And by all means, avoid using the television set as a convenient babysitter.

GUIDELINES FOR EMPLOYERS/EMPLOYEES

On occasion the situation may arise where an employer and employee are part of the same assembly. In such a case Scripture gives guidelines for both. These are stated in terms of masters and servants, or slaves, but in essence they apply to today's employer-employee relationships:

> *Servants, be obedient to them that are your masters according to the flesh, with fear and trembling, in singleness of your heart, as unto Christ;*
> *Not with eyeservice, as menpleasers; but as the servants of Christ, doing the will of God from the heart;*
> *With good will doing service, as to the Lord, and not to men:*
> *Knowing that whatsoever good thing any man doeth, the same shall he receive of the Lord, whether he be bond or free.*
> *And, ye masters, do the same things unto them, forbearing threatening: knowing that your Master also is in heaven; neither is there respect of persons with him.* (Ephesians 6:5-9)

See, also Colossians 3:22-4:1; 1 Timothy 6:1-6; Titus 2:9-10; 1 Peter 2:18-19.

These instructions are for all employers and employees. They leave no room for rebellion on the part of Christian employees against their employers, whether Christian or not. Nor do they leave room for abuse by Christian employers against their employees, whether Christian or not.

Employees who are members of labor unions are expected by both the employer and the union to abide by the bargaining contract. In the event of a strike, believers must keep the peace.

Employers should do all they can to assure that their employees—whether or not believers—receive a living wage that allows their wives to be keepers at home.

Where an employee may be an elder over his employer, he should not lord it over his employer any more than he wants his employer to lord it over him in the business world. In the assembly, all are to show kindness and love toward each other.

GUIDELINES FOR PROPERTY

It is sometimes assumed, particularly by some who separate from the mainstream, that the proper economic rule for the brethren is that all things be held in common; each is to give up his personal property for the use of "the church." The Scriptures they use to promote the idea of communal property and living are the following:

And all that believed were together, and had all things common;

And sold their possessions and goods, and parted them to all men, as every man had need.

And they, continuing daily with one accord in the temple, and breaking bread from house to house, did eat their meat with gladness and singleness of heart,

Praising God, and having favour with all the people. And the Lord added to the ekklesia daily (Acts 2:44-47)

And the multitude of them that believed were of one heart and of one soul: neither said any of them that ought of the things which he possessed was his own; but they had all things common. (Acts 4:32)

Neither was there any among them that lacked: for as many as were possessors of lands or houses sold them, and brought the prices of the things that were sold,

And laid them down at the apostles' feet: and distribution was made unto every man according as he had need. (Acts 4:34-35)

It is believed by some that Christians should not own property, but that the assembly should hold it and distribute it as it sees the need.

While this would be the ideal for a godly society, and is used as an argument by "Christian socialists," the truth is that men cannot administer such power righteously without being under absolute control by the Holy Spirit. There are several factors that applied to the early believers that do not apply today:

- These were administered by the original apostles who carried a special anointing;

- The Body of Christ was under persecution;

- There were legitimately poor people who did not have the basic needs of food, shelter and clothing. With few exceptions today, in the West especially, even the poorest have television sets, CD and DVD players, modern appliances, and other conveniences. There is no need to have all things in common;

- These actions were voluntary.

- The Scriptures tell us what took place in Jerusalem at a given time; they do not say this is a rule for all assemblies at all times.

Some might think this last statement may be said of everything in the assemblies, but this is not true. If we will keep all Scripture in proper context we will know what is for then and what is for today. Where Scripture gives definite guidelines we must hold to them.

Of course, we must be willing to give what is necessary to meet the genuine needs of others in the fellowship. And what if difficult times come upon us as they did to the first-century believers (and as they do in some places today)? It is possible that under those circumstances the Lord may lead us to sell all we have and share it with others in need. Yet He never required this even of the early believers. As Peter told Ananias and Sapphira who withheld a portion of the money from the property they sold, the property they possessed was in their own power to do with as they pleased (Acts 5:1-11). Their sin was not in withholding anything, but in lying to the Holy Spirit.

We determine what we wish to give to the Lord. We are not under obligation to tithe, but to recognize that all we have belongs to Him. Therefore, whatever we give must be given with a spirit of joy, love and generosity. Otherwise it does not please God.

GUIDELINES FOR THE MEAL

A popular custom among house assemblies today is the communal meal. This is an excellent way for the brethren to get to know one another and to share their faith.

People generally do not eat with strangers, but with those with whom they are close. When we eat together we are demonstrating our close fellowship. It is also an excellent opportunity to share the Lord's supper in the same manner in which He shared it with His apostles, and the early disciples shared it.

Scripture speaks of the "feasts" that took place when the brethren gathered together in their homes. The Lord's supper is not merely taking a piece of bread and a cup of wine or grape juice; it is a family meal. A crumb of cracker and a sip of juice can hardly be said to constitute a supper. The early believers were encouraged to eat together. Breaking bread in Scripture and in ancient cultures was a sign of fellowship. People did not eat with those from whom they were estranged. This is why Paul tells us not to eat with one who calls himself a brother in Christ but continues in open sin (1 Corinthians 5:11).

Unfortunately most of the scriptural references to the communal meal are in regard to false brethren who intrude upon the feasts. In one case, Paul chastises the Corinthian brethren for being selfish in their meals:

> When ye come together therefore into one place, this is not to eat the Lord's supper.
> For in eating every one taketh before other his own supper: and one is hungry, and another is drunken.
> What? have ye not houses to eat and to drink in? or despise ye the ekklesia of God, and shame them that have not? What shall I say to you? shall I praise you in this? I praise you not. (1 Corinthians 11:20-22)

Paul was admonishing the Corinthian brethren for coming to the Lord's supper selfishly, hoarding the food they brought. It was expected that they would come together to celebrate the Lord's supper, but they were not look upon it as just another meal. Otherwise they could have just stayed home and eaten there.

None of this negates the benefits of eating together. Paul's intent was not to have the Corinthian brethren cease from their common meal, but rather to correct their behavior. As long as they were selfish in how they ate, it was not the Lord's supper.

A personal peeve of mine is seeing the healthy, young people jump to the front of the line at buffets and stuff their plates without regard to those following behind. This is not only a problem among teenagers, but among some adults as well. In the assembly, kindness requires that deference to age and gender take precedence over personal hunger. The elderly, the women and small children should be given preference in order. This is a social rule that has been in polite society in former times, but seems to have been forgotten of late. Granted, it is not spelled out in Scripture, except in the command that the stronger should bear with the weaker. But it is a good way for young people to learn respect for their elders and to exercise some discipline over their appetites. And no one should jump in for seconds before all have had a chance to partake. If love is to be demonstrated in the common meal it would be well if we not eat for the sake of eating above the sake of fellowship. Otherwise, as Paul said, we should eat our food at home. This would be a tragedy in face of the benefits to the common meal.

Now, just what is eaten and how it is presented is open to the consensus of the brethren. Some prefer so-called "pot-luck" or "pot blessing" meals. Others prefer more formal meals, especially where the assembly is very small in number. Much depends upon the resources and the number of people involved.

We also see that the brethren combined the meal with sharing the bread and cup commemorating the Lord's death.

> *For I have received of the Lord that which also I delivered unto you, That the Lord Jesus the same night in which he was betrayed took bread:*
>
> *And when he had given thanks, he brake it, and said, Take, eat: this is my body, which is broken for you: this do in remembrance of me.*
>
> *After the same manner also he took the cup, when he had supped, saying, This cup is the new testament*

in my blood: this do ye, as oft as ye drink it, in remembrance of me.

For as often as ye eat this bread, and drink this cup, ye do shew the Lord's death till he come.

Wherefore whosoever shall eat this bread, and drink this cup of the Lord, unworthily, shall be guilty of the body and blood of the Lord.

But let a man examine himself, and so let him eat of that bread, and drink of that cup.

For he that eateth and drinketh unworthily, eateth and drinketh damnation to himself, not discerning the Lord's body.

For this cause many are weak and sickly among you, and many sleep.

For if we would judge ourselves, we should not be judged.

But when we are judged, we are chastened of the Lord, that we should not be condemned with the world.

Wherefore, my brethren, when ye come together to eat, tarry one for another.

And if any man hunger, let him eat at home; that ye come not together unto condemnation. And the rest will I set in order when I come. (1 Corinthians 11:23-34)

Breaking bread and then sharing the bread and cup in this manner cements the fellowship of the brethren. Only make sure that seating is not according to factions and favoritism as personal friends. If possible, seek out those who are lonely, feeble, or need special ministry. Love the unlovely in this aspect of fellowship and you will be filling a great void.

The early brethren were primarily Israelites, and were thus fairly close in their personal relationships; they didn't have the "privacy" factor to contend with as we in America have today.

When it comes time to share the bread and wine at the conclusion of the meal, it is incumbent upon the elders to take charge and to administer the elements. This portion of the meal should be entered into with deliberate solemnity in remembrance of the Lord's terrible sacrifice for us. But the meal in general should be a time of rejoicing and enjoying the company of our brethren, also in remembrance of the Lord's terrible sacrifice.

The practice of the early assemblies, therefore, was to come together for a meal, and at the same time honor the Lord's sacrifice. This may have been a daily occurrence, or weekly, but there is nothing in Scripture that sets a definite rule on the frequency. The important thing is that we exercise consideration and kindness toward all others in administering the meal.

Sharing dishes works better to this end than each bringing his own meal and, thus, separating himself from the rest of the brethren in practice if not in distance.

SUMMARY

Considering these rules of fellowship we are led back to the Ten Commandments. If we would obey those commandments we would find that they are based upon love for God and for our fellow man—especially our brethren in Christ.

To briefly summarize, it will be necessary to outline the Commandments rather than state them in full:

I am the LORD thy God, ... Thou shalt have none other gods before me.

We must not place on a pedestal any man or woman, or consider above God's Word anything they may teach. Many today consider their pastors as priests, representatives of God on earth in a manner that exceeds that allowed by Scripture. These priests seemingly can do no wrong. If they teach contrary to God's Word, they supplant God. And those that follow them have taken another god before the one true God.

Thou shalt not make thee any graven image, or any likeness of any thing that is in heaven above, or that is in the earth beneath, or that is in the waters beneath the earth... Thou shalt not bow down thyself unto them, nor serve them:

Images do not belong in the fellowship, no matter how "in touch with God" they may make some feel. Christian bookstores are increasingly carrying images and pictures that supposedly depict Christ, the apostles, Mary and other cannonized saints. It is becoming more and more difficult to distinquish between a Roman Catholic bookstore and a so-called "Christian" bookstore. But these images are merely the figments of men's imaginations. How can anyone paint a picture of a man and say that it represents our Lord? It would be better to rid ourselves of these things than to risk offending the One whom we claim to love.

> *Thou shalt not take the name of the LORD thy God in vain: for the LORD will not hold him guiltless that taketh his name in vain.*

How often we hear Christians use the Lord's name in vain, not as a curse word, but in careless conversation. Jokes that entail the Lord's name in any fashion are an affront to Him, as are jokes that incorporate His person. We offend the brethren when we tell such jokes or use our Lord's name carelessly.

> *Keep the sabbath day to sanctify it, as the LORD thy God hath commanded thee.*
> *Six days thou shalt labour, and do all thy work:*
> *But the seventh day is the sabbath of the LORD thy God: in it thou shalt not do any work, thou, nor thy son, nor thy daughter, nor thy manservant, nor thy maidservant, nor thine ox, nor thine ass, nor any of thy cattle, nor thy stranger that is within thy gates; that thy manservant and thy maidservant may rest as well as thou.*

This is a very personal commandment that allows for rest from labor and fellowship with the Lord. It does not necessarily mean that we must gather on the Sabbath, although that's as good a time as any to gather together. Regardless of the days we meet, we must remember not to forsake gathering together regularly for edifying and strengthening ourselves spiritually. But we must also not forget to take our rest on the Sabbath. (See the Media Spotlight special report, *Facts and Fallacies of the Resurrection: Did Jesus Really Die on Friday and Rise on Sunday?*)

> *Honour thy father and thy mother, as the LORD thy God hath commanded thee; that thy days may be prolonged, and that it may go well with thee, in the land which the LORD thy God giveth thee.*

Can we honor anyone else if we fail to honor our parents? This commandment is broken regularly, even where parents and children claim to be true believers in Christ. And the age of the children is not a factor. As long as the parents live, the children are to respect and honor them. This doesn't mean that adult children who have left their parents' home must order their lives according to their parents' wishes. But considerate behavior toward their parents must never cease.

Thou shalt not kill.

The Lord expanded on this commandment to show that if we hate another we have committed murder in our hearts. There is no place for this in the Body of Christ. Even holding resentment against someone who has injured us is sin. And we should not rejoice when trouble befalls our enemies (Proverbs 24:17-18).

Neither shalt thou commit adultery.

Adultery plagues the churches today, not just in physical relationships that betray marriages, but in lusting after other people's spouses. In this regard, it is important that all consider their dress and how it may affect others in the assembly. Young girls as well as mature women often wear clothing that barely covers the essentials. Some women excuse immodest dress with the retort, "that's their problem; they shouldn't be looking at me that way." Maybe so, but any woman who dresses in a manner that entices men is guilty of breaking the commandment she causes the men to break.

It is up to husbands to make sure their wives do not dress in a way that would entice other men. It is up to wives to obey their husbands. Fathers (and mothers) are to make sure their daughters dress modestly also. It is not uncommon to see in the churches young girls of evey age dress in ways that suggest they are young prostitutes. Is it any wonder that fornication and illegitimate births plague the churches? This ought not to be in the family of God.

Now, there are some men who want their wives to dress in a provocative manner at all times. They want to be continually enticed themselves. They would argue that it's better than looking at someone else's wife.

The truth is that they look at other men's wives as well anyway. They are so carnally minded that they do not distinquish between proper dress for others and how their wives may dress for them in the privacy of their homes. Such men do not love their wives as much as they lust for them. Godly men wish their wives to dress modestly, especially when in public. It is possible for women to dress modestly yet in a feminine fashion. While this issue is most often one of women enticing men, men cannot dress in a manner intended to entice women either. These rules apply to men's and boys clothing as well.

Love demands that in this matter, as in all matters within the assembly—and in the world for that matter—we forsake our personal desires for the benefit of others. Let us not be party to their sins.

Neither shalt thou steal.

Theft takes many forms. And there is no minimum amount of goods or money that enters into the equation. Half truths are often used to deceive and defraud another. Even pastors do not disclose everything when they attempt to get the congregation to give money for a project. Psychological ploys are used in fund raising and in getting people to act as the leaders desire. To use these ploys is to steal from God's people. Nothing less than total honesty has any room in the Body of Christ.

Theft can take the form of any half-truth, or even a truth told in a particular way to persuade someone to do for us or to give to us something we desire which he may not normally be inclined to give. Salesmen, especially, must be careful in this area.

Neither shalt thou bear false witness against thy neighbour.

Here, too, half-truths abound when stating one's case against that of another. Let us suffer loss before trying to get our way over another person.

Neither shalt thou desire thy neighbour's wife, neither shalt thou covet thy neighbour's house, his field, or his manservant, or his maidservant, his ox, or his ass, or any thing that is thy neighbour's.

Coveting anything that belongs to another is sin. Obviously, coveting another man's wife is sin. But what about coveting another man's girlfriend—or another woman's boyfriend? It is often assumed that just because no marriage vows have been stated everyone is fair game. But why bring injury to a brother's heart by stealing away someone precious to him? The rule applies in many ways beyond the obvious.

There are many other rules of fellowship that, individually, would take as much space as this general approach. Overriding all these rules is the central law that we love one another. If we will check our thoughts and actions based on that law we will find peace and harmony among the brethren. Those who break that law of love must be disciplined by the elders and taught the importance of living by it.

7
<u>The Assembly</u>

So what does take place in the Lord's assemblies? I cannot speak for all of them because I don't know exactly how they all conduct themselves. I can only speak for the assembly to which we are attached. Each segment of our gathering will be explained in as much detail as possible. This is not a formula. Each assembly must be autonomous, and must be structured on the consensus of all the brethren involved. It is merely a guide—an example of how the proper house assembly may depart from the formulaic functioning of the institutionalized congregations, and even some house churches.

THE GATHERING

To begin our gathering there is a period of fellowship and conversation among the brethren as individuals. We set a general time of 5:00 PM on the days we meet. This time of fellowship is very informal and may be likened to a social gathering. The topics of conversation among different groups of people may range from serious discussion of God's Word to social bantering. This is primarily a time for the brethren to become more intimately acquainted with one another and to enjoy each other's company. It takes place as people arrive and as those involved in preparing the meal that we enjoy together go about their work.

The Meal

In our gatherings the hostesses of the homes in which we meet provide a main course and the others bring complementary dishes, desserts, breads, etc. It's no big deal; do what comes naturally and comfortably. If a pot-blessing is more suitable for your assembly, then that's fine also. Just enjoy the fellowship around the meal. Do not think that this time requires only conversation around the Word of God. This is the best time to get to know one another without resorting to games and encounter group tactics that are more suited to strangers than to the family of God.

We do not set a length of time to eat, although we usually sit down about a half-hour after the time we first gather together. The length of time to eat is open to circumstances. While the meal is an integral part of the fellowship it is by no means the most important part.

The Bread and Cup

Immediately after the meal the male host leads us in the taking of the bread and the cup in remembrance of the Lord's death and resurrection. He may or may not read Scripture, pray, or whatever. It is up to him how he desires to commemorate the occasion. The important thing is that we are reminded of what Jesus did for us on the cross. Especially if there is someone in our midst whom we do not know well, and whose testimony of faith in Jesus may be questionable or unknown at the time, the host will remind everyone of the need to examine ourselves and to be sure that the bread and cup are taken in a worthy manner. It is up to each individual conscience whether or not to partake; no judgment is forthcoming in any case.

The elements of the portion of the Lord's supper which commemorate His death should be comprised of unleavened bread and the fruit of the grape vine.

Unleavened bread is important because it speaks of Jesus' sinlessness. To use leavened bread would be a departure from Scripture's command to use unleavened bread for the Passover meal, which we commemorate every time we eat it.

The question sometimes arises if the juice of the grape should be fermented or unfermented. Many Christians balk at the idea of using fermented wine because they have been taught that drinking alcoholic beverages is sinful, or that the fermentation process is a form of corruption. We must go to the Scriptures, not to men's ideas, to see how God looks upon alcoholic drink.

> *Wine is a mocker, strong drink is raging: and whosoever is deceived thereby is not wise.* (Proverbs 20:1)

> *An elder then must be blameless, the husband of one wife, vigilant, sober, of good behaviour, given to hospitality, apt to teach;*
> *Not given to wine, no striker, not greedy of filthy lucre; but patient, not a brawler, not covetous.* (1 Timothy 3:2-3)

> *Likewise must the deacons be grave, not doubletongued, not given to much wine, not greedy of filthy lucre.* (1 Timothy 3:8)

> *The aged women likewise, that they be in behaviour as becometh holiness, not false accusers, not given to much wine, teachers of good things.* (Titus 2:3)

There are many Scriptures which warn of the dangers of drinking too much wine or strong drink. Those warnings should be heeded. There are some Scriptures that allow for wine and strong drink. One in particular allows the Israelite to use his tithe for the Lord's feasts to consume whatever he desires, including wine and strong drink.

> *Thou shalt truly tithe all the increase of thy seed, that the field bringeth forth year by year.*
> *And thou shalt eat before the LORD thy God, in the place which he shall choose to place his name there, the tithe of thy corn, of thy wine, and of thine oil, and the firstlings of thy herds and of thy flocks; that thou mayest learn to fear the LORD thy God always.*

> *And if the way be too long for thee, so that thou art*
> *not able to carry it; or if the place be too far from thee,*
> *which the Lord thy God shall choose to set his name*
> *there, when the LORD thy God hath blessed thee:*
>
> *Then shalt thou turn it into money, and bind up*
> *the money in thine hand, and shalt go unto the place*
> *which the LORD thy God shall choose:*
>
> *And thou shalt bestow that money for whatsoever*
> *thy soul lusteth after, for oxen, or for sheep, or for*
> *wine, or for strong drink, or for whatsoever thy soul*
> *desireth: and thou shalt eat there before the LORD thy*
> *God, and thou shalt rejoice, thou, and thine*
> *household.* (Deuteronomy 14:22-26)

Whether wine used by godly men in Israel was fermented or merely grape juice is a moot point. The issue is whether or not taking any alcoholic drink is a sin. God would never even suggest we sin, so his assent to the use of strong drink should settle the issue. Although more Scriptures warn against drunkenness, we cannot play the numbers game. There is no command for total abstinence. In many countries our brethren drink wine. Do we judge them for this, contrary to God's Word?

> *Let no man therefore judge you in meat, or in drink,*
> *or in respect of an holyday, or of the new moon, or of*
> *the sabbath days:*
>
> *Which are a shadow of things to come; but the*
> *body is of Christ.* (Colossians 2:16-17)

The prohibition against wine in American Protestantism stems from the days of the temperance leagues and their effects upon American society. There is no prohibition in Scripture, only warnings against drunkenness and the consequent problems it causes. Because of the stigma attached to alcohol, especially in the United States where drunkenness is a real problem, we use grape juice in our assembly. Even though Scripture does not forbid fermented wine altogether, some who are offended by it may join us. And it's better to avoid even the appearance of what some consider evil (1 Thessalonians 5:22).

Those who disagree with these statements—who insist on either alcoholic wine or grape juice—are free to do so, but I suggest they check the Scriptures to support their argument. It is one thing to be holier-than-thou; let's not be holier than God.

Psalms, Hymns and Spiritual Songs

The institutional churches generally have a formal "music ministry" led by an accomplished or somewhat accomplished musician. Some have choirs and deck themselves in robes. There is an air of professionalism about the whole thing. Some sing traditional hymns, others opt for modern choruses—even jazz or hip hop. Whatever the style of music, the flavor is often more one of entertainment than true worship and praise.

Christians, particularly in the United States, have become accustomed to professionalism in music. This does not mean they all have good taste in music, but that they expect more than just "a joyful noise" in order to be satisfied with the time of worship and praise. Yet, fortunately, our heavenly Father has less regard for the quality of our voices and instrument-playing than He does for the condition of our hearts. There is nothing wrong with accomplished musicianship, and there's no reason why good musicianship cannot play a role in the house assembly if such musicianship is available. But it doesn't really matter how professional we sound, or whether or not we have a trained voice. We offer to God the best we have. Those offended by an occasional off-key do not have their minds stayed upon the Lord, but upon their own appetite for good music. Too bad. Tough it out and pray that the Lord will bring others into the fellowship who can supply what the rest are lacking.

Regardless of how well or poorly we do, Scripture tells us to sing unto the Lord, not with a professional leader, but as the Holy Spirit gives us the impetus to do so:

> *And be not drunk with wine, wherein is excess; but be filled with the Spirit;*
> *Speaking to yourselves in psalms and hymns and spiritual songs, singing and making melody in your heart to the Lord;*

> *Giving thanks always for all things unto God and the Father in the name of our Lord Jesus Christ.* (Ephesians 5:18-20)

> *Let the word of Christ dwell in you richly in all wisdom; teaching and admonishing one another in psalms and hymns and spiritual songs, singing with grace in your hearts to the Lord.* (Colossians 3:16)

Here we see two reasons given for a time of singing in the assembly: 1) speaking to one another, teaching and admonishing one another in songs based upon God's Word; 2) singing unto the Lord Himself, worshipping and praising Him. The idea of singing "to one another" negates the concept of a professional musician leading the congregation or conducting a choir. Choirs are more for entertainment than worship. They originated in Roman Catholicism and separate the people further from the idea that they are the Body of Christ, and they solidify the idea that "the Church" is the institution and its hierarchy. However, good musicianship produced by others is fine as long as we can focus our thoughts upon the Lord and not upon the musicians. This is not a blanket condemnation of professional musicianship within the assemblies as long as they take a very minor role. If one or more are gifted in leading in song, or can offer *a solo or two*, there is nothing wrong in it. But far better that all the brethren sing unto the Lord.

In our assembly we use hymnals as an aid in focusing on the words and learning them. Having been raised Roman Catholic or in other formal churches, or having been irreligious, many of us have not had the benefit of learning these great hymns of the Faith in our youth. And not all of the hymns are totally scriptural, so we try to use those that are. But the hymnals, as much of an aid as they are, are not essential. Someone may also sing a psalm, or a chorus learned in one of the less traditional churches in the past. One sister accompanies us on her autoharp. Another, who lives a long distance away, accompanies us on a keyboard when she can attend. At one time we had a very accomplished violinist accompany us until he moved to another state.

Other than this we have no accomplished musicians per se at this time. That does not prevent us from focusing our thoughts on the words of the songs and upon the Lord. We are encouraged by some of the words provided to us by godly men and women who have penned their music and words for the benefit of the Body of Christ.

The important thing is that we do take a time for this. But even apart from the set-apart time, it is acceptable for one to sing at any time, which prompts others to follow suit, provided they do not intrude upon the Scripture study or something else upon which the gathering is concentrating.

I should add that this is a time to refrain from banter, joking or other intrusions upon the solemnity of worship. Let us concentrate on our love and respect for our Father and Jesus.

Prayer and Sharing

This is an important time within our fellowship. It is essential to the life of the body that each member who has a need, or who knows of others' needs—whether physical, financial, emotional, or what have you—be given a forum to tell the assembly about it. This allows us all to pray in concert at that time. It also allows us to take the memory of those needs with us to continue in prayer until we gather again. We also welcome the sharing of what the Lord is doing in the lives of others both within and without our particular assembly. Maybe someone has information on something they have discerned that needs to be warned of— perhaps a news item that affects believers or the world around us, or a new religious movement. These all allow opportunities to pray or to take information that may be vital to our spiritual lives. This also is not a time for social banter. Everyone should instinctively know what is suitable for this time of sharing.

Scripture

God's Word is the center of our lives; it must also be the center of our fellowship. Even apart from any formal time in the Word, all our time together centers on Scripture. However, there is the need for teaching God's Word. In the institutional churches, a single pastor is usually the sole teacher. If he chooses, he may appoint someone to teach in his absence. However, it was never intended by the Lord to be this way. His Word clearly speaks of "elders" (plural) who are to teach:

> *The elders which are among you I exhort, who am also an elder, and a witness of the sufferings of Christ, and also a partaker of the glory that shall be revealed:*
>
> *Feed the flock of God which is among you, taking the oversight thereof, not by constraint, but willingly; not for filthy lucre, but of a ready mind;*
>
> *Neither as being lords over God's heritage, but being ensamples to the flock.*
>
> *And when the chief Shepherd shall appear, ye shall receive a crown of glory that fadeth not away.* (1 Peter 5:1-4)

Ideally, there should be more than one elder teaching. This may sometimes occur in one gathering, or different elders may take the teaching duties at different gatherings. There is no rule, but we are to be led by the Holy Spirit. In any case, a plurality of elders sharing the teaching responsibility guards against one man abusing the role of teacher and leading the assembly away from the truth. All elders and deacons are to be men. Although they may serve in other capacities, women are not to teach or take authority in the assembly:

> *Let the woman learn in silence with all subjection.*
>
> *But I suffer not a woman to teach, nor to usurp authority over the man, but to be in silence.*
>
> *For Adam was first formed, then Eve.*
>
> *And Adam was not deceived, but the woman being deceived was in the transgression.* (1 Timothy 2:11-14)

Women who teach Scripture in any congregational setting, even if that setting is made up exclusively of women, are in error. Men who allow them to teach—husbands and pastors who think they have the authority to override Scripture—are the greater sinners for allowing the women to be deceived.

It is argued, and for good reason, that there are women who are excellent teachers; they should be allowed to teach. But because someone has a natural ability to teach, it doesn't mean they are anointed by God to teach. No man should teach who is not anointed by God. And while God does anoint some men to teach, He does not anoint women to teach. That remains the province of the elders.

Understand, this prohibition extends to teaching Scripture in a congregational setting, even if it were made up of all women. It does not extend to the teaching by elder women to younger women within the context of Titus 2:3-5.

Are the women never allowed to share their knowledge of Scripture? Of course they are. First, as prophetesses. Luke 2:36 speaks of Anna, a prophetess in Israel who served God in the temple. As we look at the first-century believers we see how, as Jews, they retained in their gatherings what they knew as Jews. There is nothing in Scripture that negates the role of prophet or prophetess. On the contrary, Joel 2:28-29 prophesied that in the last days the gift of prophecy would be upon all flesh, not just the prophets of Israel. This was first confirmed at Pentecost and is recorded in Acts 2:16-19:

> *But this is that which was spoken by the prophet Joel;*
> *And it shall come to pass in the last days, saith God,*
> *I will pour out of my Spirit upon all flesh: and your*
> *sons and your daughters shall prophesy, and your*
> *young men shall see visions, and your old men shall*
> *dream dreams:*
> *And on my servants and on my handmaidens I will*
> *pour out in those days of my Spirit; and they shall*
> *prophesy.*

This confirms that the prophecy applies to the Lord's *ekklesia* for both men and women. There is a difference between teaching and prophesying. Women may prophesy, but may not teach. To claim as some do that Acts 2:17 was limited to the first-century believers is to rob the ekklesia of an important gift of the Holy Spirit that should work for the glory of God and for the edifying of the Body of Christ.

Therefore a woman in the assembly who has an exhortation to other individuals or to the assembly as a whole should be heard and judged just as any male prophet. But the judgment must be based upon the Word of God, and all prophets and prophetesses are subject to the elders.

We've already spoken of how the elder women are to teach the younger women to be keepers at home and to honor their husbands, etc. Another way women may share the Word of God is on an individual basis, even in instructing new male believers, just as Priscilla did **with her husband Aquila** in teaching Apollos about Jesus:

> *And a certain Jew named Apollos, born at Alexandria, an eloquent man, and mighty in the scriptures, came to Ephesus.*
>
> *This man was instructed in the way of the Lord; and being fervent in the spirit, he spake and taught diligently the things of the Lord, knowing only the baptism of John.*
>
> *And he began to speak boldly in the synagogue: whom when Aquila and Priscilla had heard, they took him unto them, and expounded unto him the way of God more perfectly.* (Acts 18:24-26)

So, while the scope of women teaching is very narrow, those who forbid them to share Scripture altogether are in error. The prohibition against women teachers is in any congregational setting, which is reserved for the elders.

The manner in which Scripture is taught by the elders may be different at times. There are a number of methods that may be used. The following are ways in which the elders in our assembly teach:

Systematic, verse-by-verse

The teacher reads the Scriptures, perhaps several verses, or entire chapters or more at once. He then reviews those verses one-by-one, expounding and allowing for others to share their thoughts and ask questions as the teaching progresses.

Topical

The teacher shares a Scripture on a subject, then culls from the rest of Scripture other verses that relate to the topic. As he expounds on the subject, others are allowed to share their thoughts and ask questions throughout the session.

Topical/Participating

The teacher gives others in the assembly certain Scriptures to read as the teaching progresses; he also asks them to share their thoughts on the Scriptures. All are encouraged to share their thoughts and ask questions.

You will notice that all of these methods allow for sharing and questioning by others in the assembly. This prevents the one-man-one-idea scenario. It also allows the teacher to gauge the effectiveness of his teaching, to correct any misconceptions, and to learn from others in the process.

The Women's Role

Among some brethren there is the question of how much women may participate in the time of teaching. This is a difficult issue and requires great tact to address in these days of feminist influences in the churches. Some are dogmatic for or against women having anything to say. The operational Scripture is 1 Corinthians 14:34-35:

> *Let your women keep silence in the assembly: for it is not permitted unto them to speak; but they are commanded to be under obedience, as also saith the law.*
> *And if they will learn any thing, let them ask their husbands at home: for it is a shame for women to speak in the assembly.*

It appears as if Scripture allows women to prophesy and pray, but not to teach or to disrupt a teaching by asking questions aloud. The Lord established the assembly as a male-oriented organism with the women taking part in a limited fashion: praying and prophesying. This has nothing to do with the idea that women in Israel disrupted things by shouting their questions out to their husbands across the synagogue. There is no evidence of this in Scripture or history. This belief has been a convenient tool for women to usurp the role of the men.

Being aware of this, I am nonetheless primarily concerned with taking things a little at a time. Most men who come out of the churches are relatively weak on understanding Scripture apart from what they've been taught. They are not always prepared to immediately assume the role of teacher to their wives and children. Therefore, the first step in the process is to make the brethren aware of the unscriptural forms and functioning of the establishment churches. It's much as Paul said to the Corinthian believers:

> *And I, brethren, could not speak unto you as unto spiritual, but as unto carnal, even as unto babes in Christ.*
>
> *I have fed you with milk, and not with meat: for hitherto ye were not able to bear it, neither yet now are ye able.*
>
> *For ye are yet carnal: for whereas there is among you envying, and strife, and divisions, are ye not carnal, and walk as men?*
>
> *For while one saith, I am of Paul; and another, I am of Apollos; are ye not carnal?* (1 Corinthians 3:1-4)

Most of those to whom I write are still in the churches (I am of Baptist, I am of Evangelical Free, I am of Assembly of God, etc.). While many love the Lord dearly they are yet carnal in their understanding of many important truths. Milk must be administered before solid meat. I trust the Lord will lead us to know when to say what must be said. This is also why I stressed the need for love even above form and function. The letter of the law kills, but the Spirit brings liberty.

At this time I have chosen to place the letter of the law behind the need to gently guide into an area that is terribly frightening to many—to leave the security of the establishment religious institution and begin to trust "unlearned" men led by the Spirit of God. This is a huge step for many and it behooves us to administer the rules in a manner that does not threaten the move back to biblically-based fellowship.

There are other issues I have chosen not to address just yet as well, one being the head covering for women. Suffice it to say that no rule in Scripture means anything if the people are conforming to it out of any motive other than to obey what God says in a spirit of love. I believe the Lord will reveal to individual hearts what He expects of us in every area as we draw closer to Him not only in our personal walk, but in our relationship to one another, particularly within the framework of the assembling together as His *ekklesia*.

Let us have patience with Him and with one another, and let us determine to obey no matter how much we must sacrifice.

Closing Time of Fellowship

After a time of studying Scripture together, we bring the "formal" portions of the gathering to a close with prayer. I say "formal" for lack of a better word to describe the times of essential ministry from times of general, person-to-person fellowship. The rest of the evening is spent as it began, with the brethren just enjoying one another's company. People leave as they feel led; we try not to impose upon the hosts beyond a reasonable time, but there have been times when things just kept going on their own. We gather at 5:00 PM. The earliest we tend to leave is around 10:00 PM, but we have been known to continue as late as 3:00 AM for some, while others left earlier.

Over all, the gathering of the saints should not be a time that people want to leave quickly; the ministry should be such that they are not bored or anxious to leave for something more "fun."

8
Objections

A t this point I wish to address some objections raised by those who are critical of house assemblies and believe the institutional church is the only place for believers to gather. These objections are raised by some with all good intentions. They fear for the spiritual welfare of those they love in the Body of Christ. Sometimes, however, their objections are raised out of fear of the unknown, or because of the perception that non-conventional assemblies threaten religious traditions.

NO ACCOUNTABILITY
It is argued that those who meet in houses are not accountable to proper authority; there must be a pastor who oversees the spiritual lives of the people. But to whom are most pastors accountable? To "elder boards"? Most elder boards are elected on a temporary basis and essentially work under the direction of the pastor. They are given the tasks of deacons rather than elders, being put in charge of temporal tasks within the church. In many churches the pastor is ostensibly accountable to denominational authorities. But those authorities have no intimate knowledge of the issues in the local assembly. Nor do they really know the pastor or how he conducts his business. Some consider the pastor the sole authority within the church and will back him whether or not he is wrong in his beliefs or

practices. Essentially, everyone is accountable to the pastor, but the pastor is seldom accountable to anyone else.

In the house assembly that is by its nature rather small and intimate, all are accountable to one another. Properly established, the house assembly has no single, authoritarian pastor, but is governed and taught by a plurality of elders, all of whom are accountable to one another. This is far safer and guards against error more effectively than does the traditional church scenario.

NO CREDENTIALED TEACHERS

A common question from church people is, "What are your leaders' credentials"? It is believed that one must have gone through formal seminary training in order to be qualified to teach God's Word or to oversee an assembly. Let's examine that belief.

Which credentials are valid? Every establishment church institution has its own credentials, and they do not necessarily agree on what is truth. So one credentialed "reverend" will disagree with the credentialed "most-holy reverend" of a different institution. The truth is that seminaries and Bible schools do not teach Scripture as much as they teach the *understanding* of Scripture that is held by their parent religious institution. Most pastors are well-schooled in the theological systems of their institutions, but they cannot see beyond that understanding. Credentials may prove that a person underwent the rigorous study of the institution, but they are no guarantee that that study produced knowledge of truth. The Holy Spirit is more often than not shut out of the equation. So what good are credentials when it comes to knowing God's truth?

> *But the anointing which ye have received of him abideth in you, and ye need not that any man teach you: but as the same anointing teacheth you of all things, and is truth, and is no lie, and even as it hath taught you, ye shall abide in him.* (1 John 2:27)

But if we have no need to be taught, why does Scripture allow for teachers within the assembly? This Scripture is saying that all *individual* believers are capable of knowing the truths that affect them as *individuals* without the need for formal teachers. We do not need teachers to tell us what God would have us do as individuals. But the Lord has also granted teaching as one of the ministries to the assembly at large for the edifying of the Body of Christ (Ephesians 4:11-16).

The teacher is to present truth to the assembly. But he is not a Lone Ranger. His teaching is subject to the scrutiny of not only the other elders within the assembly, but to the assembly itself. If a novice in the faith—man or woman—has an understanding of Scripture that is lacking in the most learned elder, he or she may bring that understanding to bear. It is up to the elder to submit to the truth of that understanding without regard to the less learned status of the novice. The authority for truth is not the teacher; it is God's Word rightly divided by the gifting of the indwelling Holy Spirit within all true believers in Jesus Christ. As far as credentials go, Scripture gives little regard to them:

> *For ye see your calling, brethren, how that not many wise men after the flesh, not many mighty, not many noble, are called:*
>
> *But God hath chosen the foolish things of the world to confound the wise; and God hath chosen the weak things of the world to confound the things which are mighty;*
>
> *And base things of the world, and things which are despised, hath God chosen, yea, and things which are not, to bring to nought things that are:*
>
> *That no flesh should glory in his presence.*
>
> *But of him are ye in Christ Jesus, who of God is made unto us wisdom, and righteousness, and sanctification, and redemption:*
>
> *That, according as it is written, He that glorieth, let him glory in the Lord.* (1 Corinthians 1:26-31)

Let us not forget some of the giants of the Faith who had no credentials. One, D.L. Moody, who is held in high esteem even among many church leaders, had no formal seminary training or credentials. Of course, the difference is that Moody did not challenge the church model.

In whom do many credentialed people glory? Look at their clerical robes, collars, titles and other trappings and the answer is evident.

> *Now when they saw the boldness of Peter and John, and perceived that they were unlearned and ignorant men, they marvelled; and they took knowledge of them, that they had been with Jesus.* (Acts 4:13)

Some pastors regale in the telling of this verse, critcizing the Pharisees and Sadducees for their religious pride. But they will not allow anyone who is not credentialed to hold an important position within their congregation. The truth is that not only would Peter and John (or the rest of the original twelve apostles) not be allowed to teach in today's churches, not even Jesus would meet their credentialed criteria.

In truth, if even a credentialed brother in Christ were to challenge the accepted wisdom of the pastor he would be ousted just as the credentialed apostle Paul was ousted from the synagogues. What it comes down to is not whether one has credentials but whether one rocks the boat of religious tradition regardless of the denominational origin of those traditions.

DANGER OF BECOMING A CULT

When people ask where we "go to church," we tell them that we belong to a house assembly. More often than not this takes them aback. Not wishing to be too offensive, they assume a blank look and say, "Oh. That's nice."

What's really going on in the back of their mind is "Danger! Warning! Danger! Cult!" Visions of Jim Jones and a communion of red fruit punch dance in their heads.

Christians have by-and-large been conditioned by the churches to think in terms of formal church services attended in the midst of virtual strangers as the only acceptable, safe method to gather. There is safety in familiarity and in anonymity. It has been inferred to us that we have to be careful that we not turn into a cult.

It's true that cultism is always a danger, but not only in the house assembly setting. Any religious institution that commands the loyalty of its adherents may be classified as a cult. The best defense the believer has against falling prey to a cult is a pure heart and knowledge of God's Word. Because the properly constituted house assembly encourages strong emphasis upon the Word of God and participation in the teaching of God's Word by more than one strong personality the danger of becoming a cult is less than it is in any institutional church. Any church is cultic if the pastor commands so much allegiance that the people are willing to take his (or her) word over the truth of God's Word.

DANGER OF ABUSE

Even if the house assembly doesn't become a cult, it is argued that there is a great danger of abuse from the leaders.

But why do you suppose the house assembly movement is growing? Why are so many people fleeing the churches? It is largely because of the abuse suffered at the hands of professional pastors. Abuse not only of the people, but of the Scriptures. The danger of abuse exists everywhere. But in the house assembly where there is no sole authority but a plurality of elders, the danger of abuse is far less. If anyone seeks to take over the assembly and begins asserting unwarranted authoritarianism the others will quickly put him in his place. If the attempt is serious enough he may be excluded from the assembly until he repents. No one is ensconced in his position, able to tell the dissenters to get in line with his program or take a hike.

Problems with authoritarianism are more prevalent in the churches than is realized by many believers. This is because they see only what is happening in their own church; they are not aware of how widespread these problems are. Also, many Christians are little more than outside observers to the functioning of their churches. Unless they are working to any large degree within the structure of the church they attend, most of the problems will escape their attention.

The problem that confronts those who discern these things is that they don't know where to go or what to do about it. The fear of being divisive is very genuine in these people. Such fear is induced by the clergy-laity mindset which, were we to be honest about it, is really a cultic mentality.

Many believers have "church-hopped" in the hope of finding a place where they could not only be ministered to, but which would allow them to exercise their true spiritual gifts (not the natural "talents" that many churches call spiritual gifts). They do not expect perfection, but they do expect purity of ministry and adherence to the Word of God, at least to a large extent. Some have found these things to a sufficient enough degree that they are willing to give the new church a chance. Most have found only frustration at the denigrated condition to which most of the churches have succumbed. This frustration has led many to begin seeking fellowship outside the institutional churches.

FORSAKING THE GATHERING TOGETHER

Another objection is that Scripture warns us not to forsake gathering together. We have had friends tell us just that: "You should be in a church on Sunday." To which I have replied, "Which church"? Their reply: "Any church. You shouldn't forget to gather together."

Church people generally think that if one is not sitting in a pew on Sunday morning, staring at the back of someone else's head and listening to someone talk to them from a pulpit, they are somehow failing to adhere to Hebrews 10:45. What do they think we are doing in our house assembly, ignoring one another?

What it comes down to is that only government-approved, tax-exempt churches are considered valid for gathering together. It is a subtle yet very real truth that the average Christian validates a church based upon the pastor's credentials and government-approved status. If we are not in such a church it is believed we are forsaking the fellowship of other believers. Yet there is more true fellowship and learning of Scripture to be had in one five- to eight-hour gathering in the house assembly than there is in several months of attendance at any establishment church.

Truth be known, most Christians do not want the intimacy and accountability that comes in close assembling.

NO PROGRAMS

One thing the establishment churches do offer that is lacking in the house assembly is the proliferation of peer-oriented programs. In the house assembly there is no youth ministry; children sit with their parents and learn the Word of God in a way that is perhaps above their ability to understand fully at first, but tends to help them understand better in time. The Sunday-school approach to games and watching videos of Bible "heroes" (which center on the warriors of Israel; children need "action" to keep their attention) is seldom found in house assemblies. Some house assemblies may have accommodations for infants and toddlers, but most prefer to have the children see their parents worship, pray and fellowship together, while hearing the Scriptures discussed. For that reason, just as home-schooled children are generally better educated with fewer hours of study than are government-indoctrinated or even privately-schooled children who spend more than half a day away from their parents, so children in house assemblies learn God's Word better in the company of their parents. Our only caution is that children must be kept from disrupting the proceedings.

LITTLE OR NO EMPHASIS ON GROWTH

Because the establishment churches are larger in number of members, some Christians think they are better equipped to minister to the needs of others. But size does not always equate to quality of ministry or to truth. Jesus referred to His ekklesia as a "little flock" (Luke 12:32). He also tells us that only a few will find the narrow way that leads to salvation (Matthew 7:13-14). As a general rule, if the majority of people are going east, then we should probably go west. Even among the few, the majority of the few are usually wrong, because they do not base their judgment strictly on the Word of God, but upon the Christian philosophies of men. Church programs geared toward growth are successful in bringing in the majority of the few, but they waste much in the process. Not the least wasted is the financial resources of the people.

Most of the money in church budgets goes for pastoral staff salaries, church building upkeep, maintenance and expansion, and salaries for support-staff (secretaries, grounds keepers, etc.). Within the establishment churches such things as "benevolent ministries" offer temporary material help to anyone who proves the need for it. A one-time offering may be taken to help someone get by in a time of financial need. A bag or few of groceries may be helpful to a struggling family. But there are limits set on how often and how much one may receive.

In the house assembly there are no "overhead" expenses. Our support goes directly to the brethren within the assembly who need it, without regard to how much or how often they receive. As long as the need is there, it is to be met. And we know who genuinely needs our help; there are no strangers in the house assembly. No collections are taken. The need is presented and the brethren meet it. We all recognize the need to be generous in our giving to the Lord, and we are not concerned about receiving tax deductions. We just see our priorities differently: the people, not a building or a professional clergy class, need our generosity. If no one in the assembly has a need at a particular time, we may still give to the Lord in other ways by supporting ministries that are faithful, or by giving to individuals outside the assembly—perhaps those in other assemblies—who have needs. There is no lack of opportunity to minister financially.

Much more genuine ministry may be given to individuals within the house assembly than in churches whose focus is on growth.

The issue of growth is bogus. In many cases it becomes an end in itself, often at the expense of truth. Better to split into more small assemblies wherein personal ministry may be maintained.

NO INVOLVEMENT IN THE COMMUNITY

Many churches believe they are supposed to be part of the secular community or, at least, to blend into the secular community. This has prompted many of them to invite to speak to their congregations non-believers who may blaspheme Jesus and the Father as a way of life, but who enjoy worldly prestige: mayors, governors, entertainers, sports figures and others of prominence. The idea is to show these people how nice Christians really are, and how we want to be their friends.

It's important to be friends with non-believers in order to reach them with the Gospel. Certainly it's fine for individual believers to be friends with non-believers even for social purposes, with the hope of witnessing to them. But Jesus did not establish His *ekklesia* to "fit in" to the community, or to convince non-believers how nice we can be. He tells us not to be friends with the world:

> *Love not the world, neither the things that are in the world. If any man love the world, the love of the Father is not in him.*
>
> *For all that is in the world, the lust of the flesh, and the lust of the eyes, and the pride of life, is not of the Father, but is of the world.*
>
> *And the world passeth away, and the lust thereof: but he that doeth the will of God abideth for ever.* (1 John 2:15-17)

Let us love unregenerate men, but let us not accept them into the fellowship to teach or to present awards for community service—especially if we are not winning them to Christ in the first place.

The house assembly keeps pretty much to itself. Individuals witness to others as the Lord brings them into contact. Non-believers are invited into the assembly to hear the Gospel. They have no say other than to ask questions, and may not partake of the ministries within the assembly until they make a genuine profession of faith in Jesus and exhibit sufficient spiritual growth. That is the best outreach to the community.

NO MISSIONARIES

There is always the argument that the churches, because of their size, are better equipped to send missionaries into the world.

But what is a missionary? Traditionally he is an ambassador of his institutional church. His aim may be to reach the lost in other countries for Jesus Christ, but in many cases, unless he promotes his institution's agenda and/or makes converts for the institution (which prides itself in its missionary "conquests"), he will not receive the support in the field that he needs.

Scripturally there is no such thing as a "missionary." The job of planting assemblies belongs to the apostle. But since the apostle has been dismissed by the churches, they appoint men (and women) to plant churches as extensions of their own church.

We dealt with the full aspect of the apostle's role in an earlier chapter. Suffice it to say that he is anointed by God to establish the Gospel in places where it is not found. So he also ministers as an evangelist while he plants the assembly and oversees it until it comes to maturity. He then appoints elders to lead it.

That assembly remains autonomous, not tethered to some institutional church.

Now, I am not putting down those missionaries who have sacrificed much for the Gospel. The Lord has used them and the institutions from which they came to save many souls. I am merely saying that because things have always been done a certain way doesn't mean that it is the proper or best way.

The house assembly may be started by one anointed as an apostle. He may or may not move on to establish other assemblies here or abroad. If his call is to go abroad there is nothing preventing the house assembly from supporting him in his work.

It is presumptuous to think that only large churches can take on the task of broadcasting the Gospel to other climes, especially where the large church or denomination insists on imposing its identity upon new believers.

*   *   *

The more one studies the scriptural aspects of Jesus' *ekklesia*, the more one realizes that most of the very objections raised by those opposed to the house assembly are endemic to the churches in which the objectors trust.

9
Getting Started

The urgency with which I have written this book is spurred on by the ever-increasing slide into apostasy by most of the institutional churches. The apostate Christian churches are part of the world system under Satan's control. While for centuries many Protestant and other non-Catholic churches have kept themselves from being tainted by that world system, they have been ill-equipped to stand the test of time. Each generation has further retreated from the purity of the Faith. Now, the harlot's daughters are returning to their mother:

> *And upon her forehead was a name written, MYSTERY, BABYLON THE GREAT, THE MOTHER OF HARLOTS AND ABOMINATIONS OF THE EARTH.* (Revelation 17:5)

It remains to be seen exactly who Mystery Babylon is. But the description of Babylon as a mystery to be revealed in the last days fits well that of the Roman Catholic Church out of which were spawned today's institutional Christian churches. And what does God say to His saints for that time?

> *And I heard another voice from heaven, saying, Come out of her, my people, that ye be not partakers of her sins, and that ye receive not of her plagues.*

For her sins have reached unto heaven, and God
hath remembered her iniquities. (Revelation 18:4-5)

While not all true believers will be immediately impressed to leave their churches, the time is growing short, and soon all true believers will face that decision.

It is impossible in this short treatise to discuss all the intricate instructions on gathering that are found in Scripture. Each assembly should address them on their own and learn to cope with them. The sad truth is that the Body of Christ has largely been removed from the biblical model because we have been educated in the apostate churches. For several centuries the Lord has used the churches to minister His love and truth to some degree. But as we approach the end of this age we are going to need more than just "church" to sustain us. We are going to need the true manifestation of the gifts of the Holy Spirit, not the counterfeit babble and pseudo prophecies that are all too prevalent in some of the institutional charismatic and Pentecostal churches.

We are going to need to learn to love one another, not just greet each other with the "hand of fellowship," and a "Hi, my name is Bob; glad you came to church today."

We are going to need true discipleship in learning to live godly lives, not the ungodly shepherding tactics or authoritarian insistence upon following some pastor's "vision."

All the instructions for how the assembly should function are laid out in Scripture. We must learn to implement them.

GETTING STARTED

At first it may seem a daunting task to separate oneself from the comfort of pew-warming. Because of institutional church influences, most believers feel ill-equipped to take on the role of elder or deacon in the true sense of those words. We are used to having elections guided by the pastors to fill these roles which, for the most part, are merely figurehead positions meant to rubber-stamp the pastors' desires. The role of a true elder or deacon is not that of election for a term, but appointment for life unless he proves himself unworthy at a later time.

Do not allow fear from lack of experience or intimidation from those in the churches to dissuade you. If you are seeking true biblical fellowship and you can find no one else to join you, start with your own family. Fathers are entrusted by God to teach their wives and children the Word of God. This does not mean all fathers are qualified to be elders in an assembly, but until such come along or the fathers can find a biblical assembly to join with, they should start with what they have.

As you find others of like mind to join with you, begin to establish your assembly in each other's homes. Do not try to rush things. If all the elements are not there at the beginning it doesn't really matter. Pray for the Father to increase your assembly by bringing in the gifts that it is lacking. Remember that this is a true renaissance for your faith; you must learn all over again what it means to gather in a biblical manner.

As You Grow

There are two approaches to growth within the house assembly. 1) build or rent a larger facility; 2) separate into more assemblies of manageable size. Personally, I would opt for #2. When the assemblies become too large they lose their personal approach. There is also a tendency to establish programs and separate into "peer groups." The flesh begins to think in terms of structure. Far better that the intimate fellowship continues. There is always the opportunity for the separate assemblies to meet together on occasion, perhaps for a large gathering in a park.

We are all learning anew the biblical pattern for gathering together as the *ekklesia* built by the Lord Jesus Christ. Take it slow, but be ready to move as the Holy Spirit directs.

Do not move too quickly on issues you think you understand until you have been able to address it in concert with others who possess elder and deacon qualifications. Some things must be relegated to the first-century believers if we see that they were given for a specific purpose at a specific time. Other things we must accept for the Lord's assemblies for all times.

Do not use a heavy hand on those who do not immediately understand things the way you or some of the elders understand them. Rather, with gentleness and love, guide them to the truth.

And the servant of the Lord must not strive; but be gentle unto all men, apt to teach, patient,

In meekness instructing those that oppose themselves; if God peradventure will give them repentance to the acknowledging of the truth. (2 Timothy 2:24-25)

If in the process you find they are right and you are wrong, be gracious to acknowledge your error and acquiesce to the truth.

On the other hand, overt rebellion and sin must be dealt with through a loving but firm hand. Seek God's wisdom in all things before acting. Trust the counsel of the many, but be sure that counsel is firmly grounded in the Word of God. In time, everything will come to fruition as the Lord intended, provided we are faithful to learn and practice the truth.

First, examine your own motives. Then trust the Lord to guide you into all truth and to join you with other true believers of like mind. We are merely in the beginning stages of the Lord's calling us out from among the apostate religious system. The separation will be painful, but just as birth pangs are painful but result in the birth of a loved child, so the birth pangs of true, biblical fellowship will result in a more pure form of worship and fellowship with one another and with our Father in heaven.

Avoid Identity With the Religious Establishment

There are many popular teachers in Christendom. Virtually all are part of the religious establishment in that they are leaders of, or followers of, institutional churches. While much truth may be gleaned from their teachings it behooves the leaders of the house assemblies to refrain from touting them to the assembly. To do so might create confusion and encourage the brethren to join in seminars and other gatherings that are tainted by those churches.

This isn't to say we may not fellowship with brethren who are in the churches, but wisdom dictates that we be careful to whom we give credibility.

10
A Brief Summary

I realize that what is presented in this book is a radical departure from the norm in terms of how "church" should be conducted. But, again, the properly functioning house assembly is not "church." It is, however, a true expression of how the first-century believers gathered. In summarizing, I'd like to offer a brief outline for quick reference of the highlights of this book.

The House Assembly:

- Is not a "church," "Bible study group," "cell group," or anything less than the gathering of the saints as the *ekklesia* or called-out people in Jesus Christ.

- Has no religious hierarchical structure.

- Is governed by elders who are in subjection to one another:

   Apostles
   Prophets
   Evangelists
   Shepherds
   Teachers

- Incorporates these scriptural elements:
    A common meal
    Sharing of the Lord's bread and cup
    Prayer
    Fellowship
    Psalms, hymns and spiritual songs
    Study of Scripture

- Offers the following ministries:
    The teaching of Scripture
    Holding the brethren accountable to Scripture
    Warning against spiritual deceptions
    Evangelizing the lost
    Providing fellowship
    Providing corporate worship
    Offering of prayer for one another
    The bearing of one another's burdens
    Ministering to those in need

- Is guided by the law of love

- Is authoritative, not authoritarian

- Allows for the spiritual gifts of all the brethren to be operative

- Judges sin in its midst

- Keeps the children in its midst whenever possible

The details for all these highlights are found throughout the book. It is my hope that those who read it and use it as a guide in establishing their own autonomous assembly will be as blessed as I have been. True freedom in Christ is available: freedom from the dictates of religious leaders; freedom from the need to be where we are told to be, when we are told to be there; freedom from church programs and busyness that detract from family and true fellowship in the Body of Christ. Freedom from ignorance that stunts spiritual growth.

At the same time, those who opt for the house assembly must realize that there is no room for casual Christianity if one is going to give of oneself and receive the full benefits the assembly has to offer. It is to be a close family of believers who love one another unequivocally.

Yes, there are dangers involved, but no more so—and probably even less so—than are found in most churches today.

Our growth in understanding the house assembly is gained from Scripture, but our experiences have also allowed us to put our understanding of the Scriptures to the test. As we have progressed we have changed a few things, but overall it remains a family gathering where we share a meal and the Word of God together. These, and all the other ministries in which we engage, point us to Jesus Christ as our Head, and to one another as true brethren and joint heirs with Him to the promises of God.

Appendix A
Baptism

My prayer is that you, dear reader, will come into the same full joy and understanding of the Lord Jesus Christ. Baptism is an issue which has been plagued by erroneous teachings throughout the centuries. It is important to this study on the house assembly to at least take a brief look at some of the scriptural aspects of baptism, simply because many coming from the churches into the house assembly may also bring erroneous beliefs about baptism with them. It is not my intent to do a treatise on the subject, but to point out the importance of baptism without succumbing to some form of legalism.

From the time that it was deemed a "sacrament" by the early apostate church which came to be called Roman Catholic, baptism has taken on many forms and traditions. Roman Catholicism deems baptism essential to salvation and teaches that babies who are baptized by a Catholic priest (or by a Catholic stand-in if a priest is not available) are covered for salvation until they reach "the age of reason." It also teaches that adults who are baptized into Catholicism (not into Jesus alone) receive salvation through the remittance of all their sins, including what the church calls "original sin"—the sin that plagues all mankind upon conception as the result of the fall of Adam and Eve. This approach to baptism is referred to as "baptismal regeneration"—the belief that baptism itself, being a "sacrament," or ritual which bestows God's grace by its very act, quickens a person spiritually.

To be fair, the doctrine of baptismal regeneration does require that the person enter into the sacrament by faith. The act itself does not save apart from faith. In the case of an infant, it is the Catholic faith of the parent(s) that covers the child.

Baptismal regeneration, then, is the belief that one is born again through the act of baptism as a sacrament (a means to receive grace through an act of obedience to what Roman Catholicism and other "orthodox" churches define as commands of Christ). Roman Catholicism has seven sacraments which it claims are commands of the Lord: baptism, confirmation (receiving the Holy Spirit), penance, holy communion, matrimony, holy orders and extreme unction (last rites). Episcopalian and Lutheran, as well as other "high" churches generally retain only two sacraments: baptism and holy communion.

Among some Reformed churches infant baptism is practiced not as a means for regeneration, but as a means for the child to become a member of the covenant community of believers. While this may seem reasonable, in essence it is saying that unless a child is baptized that child is not a member of the covenant community of believers. So, regardless of the denials of Reform followers, this teaching is saying that their children cannot be regarded as members of their community of believers without baptism.

In either case, there is nothing in Scripture to justify the belief in or practice of infant baptism. Scripturally, baptism follows one's confession of faith in Jesus Christ's sacrifice for the atonement of their sins. It is faith that saves before baptism is performed. In a sense, however, it is the combination of faith and baptism that confirms the confession of faith.

Now, there are those who say that baptism isn't important —that it doesn't take away sins at all. Some even refuse to baptize, believing it to be a "work" that negates the Gospel of salvation by grace alone. As usual, the truth lies between the two extremes.

Without a doubt, repentance and remission of sins, predicated upon faith in Jesus' sacrifice for the atonement of sin is the basis for one's salvation. This is the Gospel that Jesus commanded His disciples to proclaim to all nations:

> *And [Jesus] said unto them, Thus it is written, and thus it behoved Christ to suffer, and to rise from the dead the third day:*
>
> *And that repentance and remission of sins should be preached in his name among all nations, beginning at Jerusalem.*
>
> *And ye are witnesses of these things.*
>
> *And, behold, I send the promise of my Father upon you: but tarry ye in the city of Jerusalem, until ye be endued with power from on high.* (Luke 24:46-49)

Peter, in proclaiming the Gospel to Israel (with whom the New Covenant was made) states that baptism is an important element to the remission of sins:

> *Therefore let all the house of Israel know assuredly, that God hath made that same Jesus, whom ye have crucified, both Lord and Christ.*
>
> *Now when they heard this, they were pricked in their heart, and said unto Peter and to the rest of the apostles, Men and brethren, what shall we do?*
>
> *Then Peter said unto them, Repent, and be baptized every one of you in the name of Jesus Christ for the remission of sins, and ye shall receive the gift of the Holy Ghost.*
>
> *For the promise is unto you, and to your children, and to all that are afar off, even as many as the Lord our God shall call.* (Acts 2:36-39

This had nothing to do with "Old Testament" teachings for the Jews alone. It is part and parcel of Jesus' command to go into all nations and proclaim the need to be baptized for the remission of sins. Thus, if it is a command of the Lord, it is not a "work" based upon human self-righteousness. In truth, it is human self-righteousness that refuses to obey the command.

While it is important that Jesus' command be obeyed, however, baptism apart from faith is not effective. Thus, infant baptism, lacking the faith of the baptized one, is ineffective.

The question arises, what becomes of the infant that dies without baptism. What provision is there for that child?

This we leave in God's hands. Scripture does, however, allude to the child of a believing parent being holy before God:

> *For the unbelieving husband is sanctified by the wife, and the unbelieving wife is sanctified by the husband: else were your children unclean; but now are they holy.* (1 Corinthians 7:14)

Now, sanctification of the unbelieving spouse does not guarantee that unbeliever salvation. This Scripture is teaching that the unbelieving spouse is considered sacred to the marriage as long as that spouse chooses to remain with the believing spouse. In the process, God has made provision that, through the faith of the believing spouse, the child is made holy. This does not mean that the child will remain in the Faith for his life, but that he is covered by the blood of Jesus until he reaches the point in life where he can make the decision for himself whether or not to believe. Do not ask me what happens to children of two unbelievers. Scripture does not address the subject, so it would be presumptuous to say anything dogmatic about it. For all who die outside the Faith, we trust God's justice and mercy.

To summarize, whereas the doctrine of baptismal regeneration asserts that the act of baptism in faith is essential to salvation, scripturally it is the faith of the believer that is essential to salvation, and that confirmation of that salvation is in the form of baptism. The first belief places faith and baptism on equal footing; the second belief places faith before baptism. Baptism follows true faith as a sign of obedience and as a witness to one's identification with the death, burial and resurrection of Jesus:

> *Know ye not, that so many of us as were baptized into Jesus Christ were baptized into his death?*

Therefore we are buried with him by baptism into death: that like as Christ was raised up from the dead by the glory of the Father, even so we also should walk in newness of life.

For if we have been planted together in the likeness of his death, we shall be also in the likeness of his resurrection:

Knowing this, that our old man is crucified with him, that the body of sin might be destroyed, that henceforth we should not serve sin.

For he that is dead is freed from sin. (Romans 6:3-7)

God knows the heart of each believer. Because of poor teaching on the subject of baptism, many believers do not even know the necessity to be baptized as a sign of their confession of faith and as an act of obedience to Christ's command. Are they still saved? Of course. Yet I would say that, should a person confess faith in Jesus Christ, yet **refuse** to be baptized, knowing that it is a command of Christ, and knowing the significance of this act of confession before men, he is not saved. This is different than refraining from baptism through ignorance. It isn't the failure to be baptized that condemns, but the willful disobedience to Christ's commands. In other words, it is rebellion that betrays an insincere "faith" that is nothing more than either mental assent or religious belief in the fact of Christ's atonement. As James says, the devils believe and they tremble in fear (James 2:19).

Without belaboring the point, I urge the reader to study the Scriptures on the subject of baptism, first setting aside any presuppositions based upon prior teachings to which he may have been subject. Test what is said here. I have addressed baptism briefly, because I feel it is important to the life of the assembly for everyone in the assembly to be baptized with knowledge and understanding.

It isn't important who baptizes. One need not be "ordained" or even be an elder to baptize, although it would be preferable for the elders to handle that ministry. The important thing is that one understand the nature and scriptural form for baptism: immersion in water. Sprinkling (with the exception of an invalid unable to be immersed) is not baptism. The Greek word *baptizo* means "dunk" or "submerge." It does not mean "sprinkle."

As in all things of such importance we must on the one hand be firm in our convictions, and on the other hand have grace toward those who do not fully understand immediately. It is the elders' task to instruct with wisdom and meekness, yet with firmness hold the brethren to the truth of God's Word.

Appendix B
<u>Music</u>

No subject stirs controversy among Christians more than the subject of music. Even important doctrinal issues are often overlooked by some, whereas when it comes to their particular taste in music, they are ready to fight to the death in its defense. This is nowhere more evident than in the controversy over whether certain forms of music are acceptable for the believer in Christ—especially whether certain forms of music are worthy of being incorporated into Christian ministry.

Music goes back to the beginning of time. Scripture reveals that music exists in the heavenly realm. Speaking to Job of the creation of the earth, God asked,

> *Whereupon are the foundations thereof fastened? or who laid the corner stone thereof; When the morning stars sang together, and all the sons of God shouted for joy?* (Job 38:6-7)

In his lament to the king of Tyrus, which is also a prophecy to Satan, Isaiah spoke of Satan's musical qualities:

> *Thou hast been in Eden the garden of God; every precious stone was thy covering, the sardius, topaz, and the diamond, the beryl, the onyx, and the jasper, the sapphire, the emerald, and the carbuncle, and*

gold: the workmanship of thy tabrets and of thy pipes was prepared in thee in the day that thou wast created. (Ezekiel 28:13-14)

MUSIC DEFINED

What constitutes music? Is there good music and bad music? Or is it merely a matter of individual taste? And are all forms of music suitable as offerings to God?

Webster's New Collegiate Dictionary offers this definition:

> **music** ... **1a**: the science or art of ordering tones or sounds in succession, in combination, and in temporal relationships to produce a composition having unity and continuity **b**: vocal, instrumental, or mechanical sounds having rhythm, melody, or harmony **2**: an agreeable sound: EUPHONY **3** : a musical accompaniment **4**: the score of a musical composition set down on paper **5**: a distinctive type or category of music

> **musical** ... **1 a**: of or relating to music **b** : having the pleasing harmonious qualities of music;MELODIOUS **2**: having an interest in or talent for music **3**: set to or accompanied by music **4**: of or relating to musicians or music lovers

Men make all sorts of sounds with their mouths and with various objects. Yet not all objects may legitimately be classified as musical instruments. For example, typing on my computer keys produces sound. For me to call that sound "music" would be ludicrous. And while one may drum his fingers on his desk, that desk is not a musical instrument, even though it is being used as a drum for the moment.

Why? Because musical instruments are designed for the specific purpose of producing music as the term is defined. Now, objects not specifically designed to play music may be used for that purpose provided certain musical rules are applied. A washtub can be turned into a bass fiddle of sorts by using a broom handle and some different gauges of string or wire. A jug can be turned into a one-note whistle to be used as an accompaniment for other instruments. But unless non-musical instruments are either altered or used in conjunction with musical instruments, the sound they produce cannot be called music in itself.

By the same token, even the sounds made on a musical instrument are not always music. If I sat at a piano and began to run my fingers over the keys I'd never be invited to play with the London Philharmonic Orchestra. This is true because I don't know how to make music with that musical instrument.

To be classified as music, sounds must meet the particular criteria that constitute music as defined, not by anyone who thinks he knows what sounds good, but by those schooled and trained in the art and science of music.

The point is that music, being both a science (predicated upon mathematical precision of arranged notes) and an art (based upon one's ability to skillfully play those notes) is not merely what someone deems to be acceptable for listening.

The *Dictionary of the History of Ideas* (New York: Charles Scribner's Sons, 1973) indicates that, in Western civilization, impacted more than other parts of the world by the Gospel of Christ, music has often been looked upon as a gift of God:

> Music, to [Sir Thomas] Browne and many another, had in it something beyond sensuous sound to please the ear—an essential harmony that appealed even to reason and that could lead the mind to contemplation or knowledge of other things. Audible music was an image of higher kinds of harmony, that of the soul and body of man or of cosmic order, "an Hieroglyphical and shadowed lesson of the whole World, and creatures of God." If the basic principles of music were discovered, it was said, all things in the universe might be understood. Here was a key to the unchanging laws that determine the ideal concordance of unity of all that exists. And here, too, was a "gift of God" to which many might respond instinctively as well as intellectually with joy and profit.

The immutable properties of music were often said to derive from mathematical proportions that were to be found in all creation. (Vol II, p. 388)

Said Shakespeare: "Take but degree away, untone that string,/And, hark! what discord follows." (*Ibid.*)

Were I to pass the bow across my father's violin Shakespeare's observation would be evident.

Within the broad spectrum of musical possibilities, there is room for the satisfying of just about every taste. All true music meets the scientific requirements. But all things being equal in terms of ability, the degree of artistry involved in the playing of music is dependent upon the complexity of the composition. Can present-day rock and rap stand as an equal among the more complex sounds of generations gone by? Certainly the complexity of the music being rendered determines the amount of artistry involved. And today the artistry is sorely lacking.

PROGRESSION TO REGRESSION

Throughout human history music has been used by an elite few to move the souls of the masses. Music and magic have been intimately connected from earliest times.

Over the course of time music evolved, at first, to ever higher levels which required greater artistic skill on the part of the musicians. In that regard it reached its peak within Western civilization and during what may be called the era of Christian influence. The greater the understanding of God's existence and His high purpose for man, the greater man's arts and sciences flourished. That's not to say that even the civilized heathen were offering their compositions to God, but it is to say that the impact of the Gospel reached into every area of human existence to bring a quality of excellence previously unknown.

Not long after the Reformation, however, Renaissance man recognized the power of music to exalt the human spirit in the cause of humanism. The excellence of art and science, though gifts from God for man's benefit, fell victim to man's pride. Building upon the earlier excellence of those who strove to glorify God in their arts, ungodly men began to use the arts for personal profit. They recognized the impact that the arts—particularly music—can have upon human emotions. Before long, music was used less to glorify God, and more to glorify man. Gradually, as man used music for his own pleasure rather than to please God, the quality of music began to suffer. And the purpose of music has, for the masses, appealed more and more to the base nature of sin. Having risen from the primitive sounds of the heathen, music (as has all art) began to regress to those primitive roots.

Christians must consider carefully the role music plays in their attitudes, feelings and actions. It is especially necessary to consider whether some forms of music are suitable for offering to God in the area of worship and praise.

Let me say that, in my flesh, I enjoy all types of true music. I do not enjoy rap, punk, metal or other cacophonous noises which media profiteers pass off as "music." By all the rules of music, these are not music—certainly not music of a high order. I realize some will disagree, but so be it. Yet, for the purposes of this writing, I will allow them to be classified as music so that we may deal with them for the issues involved.

TO WHAT SHOULD WE LISTEN ?

If there is one area of dispute to which most of us can identify, it is the dispute between parents and children as to what kind of music is allowed in the home. Ever since music became popularized through the mass media—radio and phonograph records to start; videos and CDs at present—this dispute has raged from generation to generation. The turn of the century saw what parents at that time considered corruptible music such as ragtime. Those brought up on ragtime were horrified at the more promiscuous music and dancing styles of the twenties and thirties. During the forties, music began to move toward a more primitive style. Drums and rhythm sections began to dominate the big band era. Parents at that time forgot how they had brought consternation upon their own parents with their popular music.

The fifties saw a dramatic turn toward not only more primitive and sensuous music and dancing, but toward a decline in musicianship. Whereas the big bands still required excellence of musicianship, small groups were used more and more as supporting roles for popular vocalists. Soon, the most popular groups consisted of nothing more than guitars and drums. At the same time, the primitive, soulish music carried a more promiscuous message that came through not only in the lyrics, but in the sound itself. The drug culture of the sixties made psychedelia the "in thing." And, again, parents, whose worst vices may have been drinking alcohol and smoking, were dismayed at the increase in the use of illegal drugs. True, drug use was popular among musicians, artists and other creative people for decades prior to the sixties, but among the masses, drugs were still largely considered taboo. A high school junkie in the fifties was shunned and whispered about.

The seventies saw an even greater move away from musical skills and toward licentious expression. What passed as music was used more and more with drugs to induce a hypnotic stupor —an escape from reality into a world of depression, anger and rebellion against established authority. Since that time, the music of the eighties and nineties has built more intensely upon those themes. Today, gangsta rap and hip hop, the most primitive sounds yet, have become some of the most popular. And the messages that accompany these sounds are anger, hatred and despair.

Those who promote these sounds say they are the expressions of today's youth, fed up with the disparity of wealth between the haves and have-nots. But if that's the message, then that same message can be conveyed with more musical skill. It isn't just the message; the beat works to stir up the anger and hatred. The repetitive, staccato-like verses of rap are the sounds of jungle warriors preparing for battle. And the attitude is often one of total disregard for human life and property. As for the disparity of wealth, today's "musicians" make (I won't say "earn") obscene amounts of money for their talentless productions.

As each generation has fulfilled Satan's purpose in bringing man to the brink of destruction and mindlessness so that he can be controlled by the "world servers" for the New World Order, parents have justifiably been concerned. Yet many overlook the obvious differences in generational attitudes. The excuse often heard for this is, "Well, we had our music and we turned out okay; I guess our kids will survive this music." But did we turn out okay? Are we, as a generation, closer to God than our parents' generation? Or are we farther away? Was our parents' generation closer to God than their parents' generation? Or were they farther away?

I believe that each generation has moved farther from God. This is apparent not only in the spiritual condition of each succeeding generation, but especially in the spiritual condition of the churches. When we read the profound spiritual writings of our brethren from before the turn of the century back to the time of the Reformation, we see a quality of godliness seldom evidenced by today's Christian authors. Each succeeding generation has become more and more absorbed in self, and the writings of each generation attest to the spiritual vacuum and lukewarm attitudes of today's churches.

With few exceptions (notably drinking songs to the tune of fraternal worship), prior generations would never have thought to incorporate their worldly music into Christian worship. So why are today's sounds, including satanic-inspired sounds, used in such a way? The answer is that prior generations knew instinctively that there is the world's music and music suitable for the Body of Christ, and they are mutually exclusive. They did not insist that their favorite worldly music be incorporated into their worship. That distinction has been lost to the present generation because, as a whole, it is farther from God.

I'm not saying there are no godly young people today; I am saying their judgment has been clouded by the world's influence. The mass media did not have near the influence upon the minds of past generations as they do today.

WHO'S TO JUDGE?

It may be rightly argued that I am no better a judge of what God wants than anyone else. I cannot tell you that, according to my authority, the music I like is what God likes, and the music you like is what God dislikes. So who is to judge what we should offer to God?

To be honest, we must admit that our arguments for or against a particular type of music is based on what we've been sold as a generation. People are no different today than they were six thousand years ago. Tastes in music and other things are acquired; they are not inbred. Any of us—were we born just prior to the seventies—would most likely be fans of hard rock. Were we born just prior to the twenties, we'd dance the Charleston. To argue otherwise would be to say that each generation is endowed with certain likes and dislikes from conception—especially Americans. Did the human race all of a sudden like rap and hip hop? Or is their popularity the result of exploitation by the media?

We like what we've been fed from an early age. Although with maturity some tastes change, in general we follow the mass cultural standards for our time. And the people feeding us those standards know how to manipulate us for their personal gain. Most things become time-worn. In order to keep the money coming in, new things must take their place. How can one improve upon the masters of classical music? They can't. So it becomes necessary to produce a different sound. Who can improve upon the great artistry of the big band era? No one. So it becomes necessary to produce yet a different sound. The bottom line being monetary profit, the less expensive it is to produce the product, the more profit can be made. Artistry does not come cheap; the primitive beat does. All these factors considered, the tastes of the previous generation must be deemed "out," and the current tastes fed to each succeeding generation by the media profiteers must be deemed "in." The problem is that, without improvement, there must be degeneration. There is no other way to go.

Since taste is thus induced—especially since it is induced largely by unregenerate men—no one, regardless of age, can argue for their particular taste when it comes to what is acceptable to God.

The only source to which we can look for guidance is God's Word. Whatever Scripture says about music is what we are to hold to, regardless of our particular taste. The problem is that God's Word doesn't say a whole lot about musical styles. In fact, it doesn't say a whole lot about music. This doesn't mean, however, that music is unimportant to God. All the Scripture verses pertaining to music relate to worship and praise of God. Musical instruments and the human voice are to be used for this purpose. Does this mean that all other music should be forbidden? At one time, and among certain sects of Christianity, certain music was forbidden. It still is among some. But Scripture doesn't forbid us from using music for other purposes. What is more important than the music itself is the attitude of the person playing or listening to it.

That being the case, some may argue for all sorts of musical styles, provided the heart's attitude is proper. Not necessarily. Regardless of motive, particular forms of music induce specific emotions and feelings in people. Some of those emotions and feelings are not conducive to holiness.

Those who write musical scores for movies know the psychology of music and how certain kinds of music may be used to create feelings that draw the viewer into the plot of the film. Alfred Hitchcock's *Psycho* utilized a screaming synthesizer which induced fear as Norman Bates plunged his knife into his victims. Similar techniques are used in all horror movies in order to convey the message of danger and fear. There is music for suspense, action, sorrow, romance, demonism and every emotion known to man.

Military personnel will attest that a military march induces feelings of power and unity with one's comrades in arms. Governments know which sounds stir patriotism and can use them to move the masses to support their schemes. Calls to patriotism are seldom more than calls to support for a particular government's power. The secret is to fool the masses into thinking they are being "patriotic." Music serves that purpose well.

Romantic themes utilize violins and other stringed instruments in compositions designed to produce feelings of tranquility and love. Western music is easily identified, as is that used for heavy drama. So, too, is sexually stimulating music, and bawdy music. David Rose's *The Stripper* conveys the same message whether or not you know the title of the tune. Most importantly, music from the past few decades, especially, is designed to instill feelings of agitation, anger and rebellion. It caters to the desire of all sinful flesh to be free of the control of others, including God.

No one who knows anything about these matters can deny this. Our minds immediately identify with the emotions conveyed through various forms of music.

The reason most Christians think musical taste is unimportant is that they do not understand that the laws which govern music are created by God. They can be used as God intended, or they can be used as man intends.

Certainly there is a heavenly music—a style which characterizes holiness. Can one say that just any kind of music is suitable for offering to God? Can we imagine rock, rap or even big band jazz being played before God's throne? Of course not. Not because these do not fall within the spectrum of music, but because the feelings and messages they convey by their very nature are soulish, not spiritual.

The heavenly form of music can be approached here on earth. Just as we can identify the emotions conveyed through secular music, when it comes to music that exalts God we likewise immediately identify it as worshipful. While the patterns may vary some, the quality of music for worship and praise falls within a narrow band that lifts the spirit, not just the soul, and exalts God in its measure.

The apostle Paul tells us that, whatever we do, we should do all to the glory of God (1 Corinthians 10:31). And even though Scripture is silent on musical style, we instinctively know what should be used to glorify God. As much as I enjoy big band music, I must admit that such music is not suitable for worship or praise. It lifts the soul but not the spirit. That's not to say that all worldly music is evil in itself; it is to say that it is not conducive to spiritual edification.

May we still enjoy it? I believe so. Just as eating and drinking are not always for nutrition but for pleasure, so different music may be enjoyed as long as the thoughts and emotions it engenders are not sinful, or it doesn't lend itself to the appearance of evil. This applies to all forms of music that are soulish in nature, including that through which the artists may claim they are glorifying God. Because one says one is glorifying God doesn't mean one is glorifying God. The only way we can truly glorify God is to live in obedience to His Word. And that obedience applies to the way we use music in our service to Him. This is where the Holy Spirit gives guidance.

All our service to God must be prompted by God's Spirit. Otherwise we are offering strange fire, coming from our own volition. We are producing wood, hay and stubble, rather than gold, silver and precious stones. We may accomplish many mighty works; we may produce great musical quality; we may use the proper words that should exalt God in our vocals. But if our service is of the flesh it will reflect the works of the flesh and will not please God. And it doesn't matter how many testimonials, or how many "Angel Awards" we receive. We are only fooling ourselves and leading the brethren astray.

Therefore, if our worship is to be given through the prompting of the Holy Spirit, it stands to reason that all we do in the Spirit will reflect the fruit of the Spirit. And what are the works of the flesh as opposed to the fruit of the Spirit? Paul sums it up:

> *Now the works of the flesh are manifest, which are these; Adultery, fornication, uncleanness, lasciviousness,*
>
> *Idolatry, witchcraft, hatred, variance, emulations, wrath, strife, seditions, heresies,*
>
> *Envyings, murders, drunkenness, revellings, and such like: of the which I tell you before, as I have also told you in time past, that they which do such things shall not inherit the kingdom of God.*
>
> *But the fruit of the Spirit is love, joy, peace, longsuffering, gentleness, goodness, faith,*
>
> *Meekness, temperance: against such there is no law.*
>
> *And they that are Christ's have crucified the flesh with the affections and lusts.* (Gal. 5:19-24)

Consider the quality (or lack thereof) of your favorite music—especially music from the past few generations. Does it reflect humility—the mind of Christ? Does it reflect love, joy, peace, patience, gentleness, goodness, faith, or any of the other qualities of the fruit of the Spirit? If not, it may appeal to the soul, it may sound pleasant to our ears, but it is not suitable for the spiritual worship of God.

Some might argue that their music speaks of love and joy. And that may sometimes be true, in the human sense, although "love" is often confused with "lust." But the fruit of the Spirit is one fruit; it is not a pick-and-choose smorgasbord. We cannot choose love and joy and neglect the humility which the other qualities of the fruit express. True love and joy are inseparable from patience, peace, gentleness, etc.

To use music that expresses the works of the flesh as an offering to God shows contempt for God's majesty. Although the music may in itself be neutral toward righteousness, or may even express in words one's love of God, it is still soulish. By insisting on its use for worship, praise or spiritual edification we tell God that we want to please our soulish nature rather than to please Him. We allow our disputes with other men over individual tastes of the flesh to intrude into our spiritual service.

If we have been crucified with Christ, then we are dead to our fleshly desires. This doesn't mean they don't exist. They are not dead; we are. But they continue to plague us as long as we reside in this sinful flesh. Our spirits and souls have been redeemed, but our flesh is very much alive. And our souls—that element of our consciousness which must weigh the desires of the flesh against the desires of God's Spirit within us—is often torn between pleasing God and pleasing self. Even though our soul has been saved, it can only act in accordance with the light that it has received. And the only light God has given us is His Word. As we study the Scriptures, His Spirit illumines our minds (our souls) and convicts us of our sins and errors. It is up to us to respond in obedience to that conviction. God has set the standard, and all arguments should cease.

PARENTS VS CHILDREN

Especially in the disputes between parents and their children, arguments should cease. Children who argue that their ways are different from their parents' ways may be technically correct. But it isn't a matter of whose way is right. There is only one Way, and that is God's Way.

Now, since God demands that children obey their parents, there should be no argument from the children. They are to obey their parents regardless of their own desires except in cases where they are commanded to sin. And it doesn't matter who is technically right.

> *Children, obey your parents in the Lord: for this is right.* (Ephesians 6:1).

That's all there is to it. There need be no strife in households if children will obey their parents. Abusive parents aside, if there is strife among parents and children the children are wrong, period.

CONCLUSION

While God's Word tells us to live in the Spirit, many producers of contemporary Christian music cater to the flesh. Like the world, they know where the profits lie. This is why some of the best, most worshipful music is the least expensive. It isn't in as much demand. Also, the Christian media (much of which is owned by non-believers) mimic each generation's particular secular sounds in order to get the most dollars out of the Christian market.

The enemy of our souls has conned us into thinking that anything is acceptable to God if we are convinced in our own minds that it is offered out of a motive of love. While motive is important, God tells us that obedience is better than sacrifice. Saul's motive in offering his strange fire was, in his own mind at least, pure. But he disobeyed the clear instruction of God's prophet. So, too, many Christians offer strange fire thinking they are doing God a service. When the Day of the Lord comes and every work is tried by fire, they will be sorely disappointed to find that they were really serving their own flesh.

TO ORDER SWORD PUBLISHERS BOOKS

Send check, money order or credit card information to:

SWORD PUBLISHERS
P.O. BOX 290
REDMOND, WA 98073

Or order on-line at www.swordpublishers.com

You may also receive Media Spotlight's journal and special reports without cost or obligation by writing to the above address.

The current issue will be sent to you. In it you will find a catalog of all available reports on various topics of critical importance to the body of christ.

See the next page for information on Media Spotlight Ministries.

ORDER FORM FOR SWORD PUBLISHERS

Quantity	Title		Amount
_____	What Do You Believe?	$14.00/ea	$_____
_____	Vengeance Is Ours	$10.00/ea	_____
_____	The World Christian Movement	$14.00/ea	_____
_____	The House Assembly	$12.00/ea	_____
	Canada & Mexico Add $3US Shipping per book		_____
	All Other Foreign Add $5US Shipping per book		_____
		SUB-TOTAL	_____
	Washington Residents Add 8.8% Tax on Sub-Total		_____
		TOTAL $	_____

☐ Check/M.O. Enclosed

Please charge my ☐ Visa ☐ MasterCard

#_____

Expiration Date_____

Name_____

Address_____Phone(____)_____

City_____ State_____ Zip_____

Those who order books from Sword Publishers will also receive Media Spotlight's journal and special reports without cost or obligation.

WHO IS MEDIA SPOTLIGHT?

Media Spotlight brings understanding of the ways in which the world shapes our thinking and lifestyles, particularly through the influence of the mass media, both secular and religious.

Because God's Word exhorts us to "buy the truth and sell it not" (Prov. 23:23), we do not sell our periodical publications. Nor do we carry advertising in order to avoid outside influences.

When Media Spotlight began in 1977, we were the first ministry on a national scale to specifically address the ungodly nature of the secular media, particularly motion pictures, television, toys, games and myriad other problems that contribute to Christians living no differently than the world.

The mass media have impacted the Body of Christ as much as they have society. Many Christians are so dependent upon the media that they aren't aware of how lukewarm they have become. We have many testimonies from readers who tell us that, because of Media Spotlight, they no longer compromise their love for God with the need to be entertained. They have become aware of the effect the media have on their thinking, and are now more selective in their choices.

But the problem of ungodliness is not exclusive to the secular media. The religious media also present messages contrary to God's Word. We address religious teachers that impact believers in Christ, whether for good or for evil.

It has escaped the understanding of many Christians that what they believe is more often shaped by the teachings and traditions of religious men and institutions than by Scripture. Yet the wisdom of the world is no substitute for God's Word, even if offered from the pulpit or in the Christian media.

Jesus warned us that in the last days false Christs and false prophets would arise and would show great signs and wonders, "insomuch that, if it were possible, they shall deceive the very elect." He also said that, at the same time, the love of many toward Him would grow cold because evil would increase in the world. If we believe Him, then we would be foolish not to guard ourselves against deception. There is little time to waste in the short span of life granted us by God. We must choose today whom we will serve.

MEDIA SPOTLIGHT
P.O. Box 290 - Redmond, WA 98073-0290

TO ORDER SWORD PUBLISHERS BOOKS

Send check, money order or credit card information to:

SWORD PUBLISHERS
P.O. BOX 290
REDMOND, WA 98073

Or order on-line at www.swordpublishers.com

You may also receive Media Spotlight's journal and special reports without cost or obligation by writing to the above address.

The current issue will be sent to you. In it you will find a catalog of all available reports on various topics of critical importance to the body of christ.

See the next page for information on Media Spotlight Ministries.

ORDER FORM FOR SWORD PUBLISHERS

Quantity	Title	Amount
_____	What Do You Believe?	$14.00/ea $_____
_____	Vengeance Is Ours	$10.00/ea _____
_____	The World Christian Movement	$14.00/ea _____
_____	The House Assembly	$12.00/ea _____
	Canada & Mexico Add $3US Shipping per book	_____
	All Other Foreign Add $5US Shipping per book	_____
	SUB-TOTAL	_____
	Washington Residents Add 8.8% Tax on Sub-Total	_____
	TOTAL $	_____

☐ Check/M.O. Enclosed

Please charge my ☐ Visa   ☐ MasterCard

#_____

Expiration Date_____

Name_____

Address_____Phone(____)_____

City_____ State_____ Zip_____

Those who order books from Sword Publishers will also receive Media Spotlight's journal and special reports without cost or obligation.

WHO IS MEDIA SPOTLIGHT?

Media Spotlight brings understanding of the ways in which the world shapes our thinking and lifestyles, particularly through the influence of the mass media, both secular and religious.

Because God's Word exhorts us to "buy the truth and sell it not" (Prov. 23:23), we do not sell our periodical publications. Nor do we carry advertising in order to avoid outside influences.

When Media Spotlight began in 1977, we were the first ministry on a national scale to specifically address the ungodly nature of the secular media, particularly motion pictures, television, toys, games and myriad other problems that contribute to Christians living no differently than the world.

The mass media have impacted the Body of Christ as much as they have society. Many Christians are so dependent upon the media that they aren't aware of how lukewarm they have become. We have many testimonies from readers who tell us that, because of Media Spotlight, they no longer compromise their love for God with the need to be entertained. They have become aware of the effect the media have on their thinking, and are now more selective in their choices.

But the problem of ungodliness is not exclusive to the secular media. The religious media also present messages contrary to God's Word. We address religious teachers that impact believers in Christ, whether for good or for evil.

It has escaped the understanding of many Christians that what they believe is more often shaped by the teachings and traditions of religious men and institutions than by Scripture. Yet the wisdom of the world is no substitute for God's Word, even if offered from the pulpit or in the Christian media.

Jesus warned us that in the last days false Christs and false prophets would arise and would show great signs and wonders, "insomuch that, if it were possible, they shall deceive the very elect." He also said that, at the same time, the love of many toward Him would grow cold because evil would increase in the world. If we believe Him, then we would be foolish not to guard ourselves against deception. There is little time to waste in the short span of life granted us by God. We must choose today whom we will serve.

MEDIA SPOTLIGHT
P.O. Box 290 - Redmond, WA 98073-0290